HISTORY OF CANADIAN LITERATURE

HISTORY
OF
CANADIAN LITERATURE

P. K. Sinha
Jagdish K. Ghosh

Commonwealth

History of Canadian Literature

Edition : 2021

ISBN 978-81-311-0323-4

Published by :
COMMONWEALTH PUBLISHERS PVT. LTD.
4831/24, Prahlad Street,
Ansari Road, Darya Ganj,
New Delhi - 110002
Ph. : 23275511, 23257835
e-mail : commonwealthbooks@gmail.com

Laser Typesetting by :
Rishu Computers
Delhi

Printed at :
Roshan Offset Printers
Delhi

Preface

Canada's literature, whether written in English or French, often reflects the Canadian perspective on nature, frontier life and Canada's position in the world, all three of which tie in to the garrison mentality. Canada's ethnic and cultural diversity are reflected in its literature, with many of its most prominent writers focusing on ethnic life.

While Canadian literature, like the literature of every nation state, is influenced by its socio-political contexts, Canadian writers have produced a variety of genres. Influences on Canadian writers are broad, both geographically and historically. Canada's dominant cultures were originally British and French, as well as aboriginal. The country's literature has been strongly influenced by international immigration, particularly in recent decades.

The present book comprehensively explains the historical development of Canadian literature. It aims to provide education, entertainment and enlightenment to the readers. It is intended for advanced level students of literature, who are taking exams or modules in this field. It may also be suitable for teachers, researchers and the general reader who is interested in the history of literature.

Authors

Contents

1

Introduction to Canadian Literature

Canada is a country occupying most of northern North America, extending from the Atlantic Ocean in the east to the Pacific Ocean in the west and northward into the Arctic Ocean. It is the world's second largest country by total area and its common border with the United States to the south and northwest is the longest in the world.

The land occupied by Canada was inhabited for millennia by various groups of Aboriginal people. Beginning in the late 15th century, British and French expeditions explored, and later settled along, the Atlantic coast. France ceded nearly all of its colonies in North America in 1763 after the Seven Years' War.

In 1867, with the union of three British North American colonies through Confederation, Canada was formed as a federal dominion of four provinces. This began an accretion of provinces and territories and a process of increasing autonomy from the United Kingdom. This widening autonomy was highlighted by the Statute of Westminster of 1931 and culminated in the Canada Act of 1982, which severed the vestiges of legal dependence on the British parliament.

Languages

Canada's two official languages are English and French. Official bilingualism is defined in the Canadian Charter of Rights and Freedoms, the Official Languages Act, and *Official Language Regulations*; it is applied by the Commissioner of Official Languages. English and French have equal status in federal courts, Parliament, and in all federal institutions. Citizens have the right, where there is sufficient demand, to receive federal government services in either English or French, and official-language minorities are guaranteed their own schools in all provinces and territories.

English and French are the mother tongues of 59.7% and 23.2% of the population respectively, and the languages most spoken at home by 68.3% and 22.3% of the population respectively. 98.5% of Canadians speak English or French (67.5% speak English only, 13.3% speak French only, and 17.7% speak both). English and French Official Language Communities, defined by First Official Language Spoken, constitute 73.0% and 23.6% of the population respectively.

Although more than 85% of French-speaking Canadians live in Quebec, there are substantial Francophone populations in Ontario, Alberta, and southern Manitoba. New Brunswick, the only officially bilingual province, has an Acadian population constituting 33% of the population. There are also clusters of Acadians in southwestern Nova Scotia, on Cape Breton Island, and through central and western Prince Edward Island. Ontario has the largest French-speaking population outside Quebec. The Charter of the French Language makes French the official language in Quebec.

Other provinces have no official languages as such, but French is used as a language of instruction, in courts, and for other government services in addition to English. Manitoba, Ontario, and Quebec allow for both English and French to be spoken in the provincial legislatures, and laws are enacted in both languages. In Ontario, French has some legal status but is not fully co-official. Several aboriginal languages have official status in the Northwest Territories. Inuktitut is the majority language in Nunavut, and one of three official languages in the territory.

Literature

Canadian literature may be divided in two parts, somewhat like a tree with two great roots. One root is the deeply buried culture of France. The other is just as deeply buried in the traditions of England. One part of Canadian literature is written in French, the other in English. But the branches of this tree are purely Canadian. Authors and readers of each literature are gaining more and more knowledge of the other, in the original or in translation.

Canada's literature, whether written in English or French, often reflects the Canadian perspective on:

1. Nature,
2. Frontier life, and
3. Canada's position in the world, all three of which tie in to the garrison mentality. Canada's ethnic and cultural diversity are reflected in its literature, with many of its most prominent writers focusing on ethnic life.

Because of its size and breadth, Canadian literature is often divided into sub-categories.

1. The most common is to categorize it by region or province.
2. Another way is to categorize it by author. For instance, the literature of Canadian women, Acadians, Aboriginal peoples in Canada, and Irish Canadians have been anthologized as bodies of work.
3. A third is to divide it by literary period, such as "Canadian postmoderns" or "Canadian Poets Between the Wars."

Traits common to works of Canadian literature include:

1. *Failure as a theme*: Failure and futility feature heavily as themes in many notable works; for instance, *Not Wanted on the Voyage* by Timothy Findley or *Kamouraska* by Anne Hebert.
2. *Humour*: Serious subject matter is often laced with humour.
3. *Mild anti-Americanism*: There is marked sentiment of anti-American often in the form of gentle satire. While it is sometimes perceived as malicious, it often presents a friendly rivalry between the two nations
4. *Multiculturalism*: Since World War Two, multiculturalism has been an important theme. Writers using this theme include Mordecai Richler (known for novels such as *The Apprenticeship of Duddy Kravitz*), Margaret Laurence (known for novels such as *The Stone Angel*), Rohinton Mistry, Michael Ondaatje — The English Patient— *and prolific Chinese Canadian writer Wayson Choy.*
5. *Nature (and a "human vs. nature" tension):* Reference to nature is common in Canada's literature.

Nature is sometimes portrayed like an enemy, and sometimes like a divine force.

6. *Satire and irony:* Satire is probably one of the main elements of Canadian literature.
7. *Self-deprecation:* Another common theme in Canadian literature.
8. *Search for Self-Identity:* Some Canadian novels revolve around the theme of the search for one's identity and the need to justify one's existence. A good example is Robertson Davies's *Fifth Business,* in which the main character Dunstan Ramsay searches for a new identity by leaving his old town of Deptford.
9. *Southern Ontario Gothic:* A sub-genre which critiques the stereotypical Protestant mentality of Southern Ontario; many of Canada's most internationally famous authors write in this style.
10. *The underdog hero*: The most common hero of Canadian literature, an ordinary person who must overcome challenges from a large corporation, a bank, a rich tycoon, a government, a natural disaster, and so on.
11. *Urban vs. rural*: A variant of the underdog theme which involves a conflict between urban culture and rural culture, usually portraying the rural characters as morally superior. Often, as in Stephen Leacock's *Sunshine Sketches of a Little Town* or Alistair MacLeod's *No Great Mischief,* the simplicity of rural living is lost in the city.

In 1802, the Lower Canada legislative library was founded, being one of the first in Occident, the first in the Canadas. For comparison, the library of the British house of commons was founded sixteen years later. It should be noted the library had some rare titles about geography, natural science and letters. All books it contained were moved to the Canadian parliament in Montreal when the two Canadas, lower and upper, were united. On April 25, 1849, a dramatic event occurred: the Canadian parliament was burned by furious people along with thousands of French Canadian books and a few hundred of English books. This is why some people still affirm today, falsely, that from the early settlements until the 1820s, Quebec had virtually no literature. Though historians, journalists, and learned priests published, overall the total output that remain from this period and that had been kept out of the burned parliament is small.

It was the rise of Quebec patriotism and the 1837 Lower Canada Rebellion, in addition to a modern system of primary school education, which led to the rise of French-Canadian fiction. *L'influence d'un livre* by Philippe-Ignace-Francois Aubert de Gaspé is widely regarded as the first French-Canadian novel. The genres which first became popular were the rural novel and the historical novel. French authors were influential, especially authors like Balzac.

In 1866, Father Henri-Raymond Casgrain became one of Quebec's first literary theorists. He argued that literature's goal should be to project an image of proper Catholic morality. However, a few authors like Louis-Honoré Fréchette and Arthur Buies broke the conventions to write more interesting works.

This pattern continued until the 1930s with a new group of authors educated at the Université Laval and the Université de Montréal. Novels with psychological and sociological foundations became the norm. Authors such as Gabrielle Roy and Anne Hébert, for the first time, began to earn international acclaim. During this period, Quebec theatre, which had previously been melodramas and comedies, became far more involved.

French-Canadian literature began to greatly expand with the turmoil of the Second World War, the beginnings of industrialization in the 1950s, and most especially the Quiet Revolution in the 1960s. French-Canadian literature also began to attract a great deal of attention globally, with Acadian novelist Antonine Maillet winning the Prix Goncourt. An experimental branch of Québécois literature also developed; for instance the poet Nicole Brossard wrote in a formalist style. In 1979, Roch Carrier wrote the story *The Hockey Sweater,* which highlighted the cultural and social tensions between English and French speaking Canada.

Contemporary Canadian Literature

Following World War II, writers such as Mavis Gallant, Mordecai Richler, Norman Levine, Margaret Laurence and Irving Layton brought added to the Modernist influence to Canadian literature previously introduced by F.R. Scott, A.J.M. Smith and others associated with the *McGill Fortnightly.* This influence, at first, was not broadly appreciated. Norman Levine's *Canada Made Me,* a travelogue that presented a sour interpretation of the country in 1958, for example, was widely rejected.

After 1967, the country's centennial year, the national government increased funding to publishers and numerous small presses began operating throughout the country.

In the late 1970s, science fiction fan and scholar of Canadian literature Susan Wood helped pioneer the study of feminist science fiction, and (along with immigrant editor Judith Merril) brought new respectability to the study of Canadian science fiction, paving the way for the rise of such phenomena as the French-Canadian science fiction magazine *Solaris*.

By the 1990s, Canadian literature was viewed as some of the world's best.

Canadian authors have accumulated international awards:

1. In 1992, Michael Ondaatje became the first Canadian to win the Booker Prize for *The English Patient*.
2. Margaret Atwood won the Booker in 2000 for *The Blind Assassin* and Yann Martel won it in 2002 for *Life of Pi*.
3. Alistair MacLeod won the 2001 IMPAC Award for *No Great Mischief* and Rawi Hage won it in 2008 for *De Niro's Game*.
4. Carol Shields's *The Stone Diaries* won the 1995 Pulitzer Prize for Fiction, and in 1998 her novel *Larry's Party* won the Orange Prize.

Notable Figures

Because Canada only officially became a country on July 1, 1867, it has been argued that literature written before this time was colonial. For example, Susanna Moodie and Catherine Parr Traill, English sisters who adopted the country as their own, moved to Canada in 1832. They recorded their experiences as pioneers in Parr Traill's *The Backwoods of Canada* (1836) and *Canadian Crusoes* (1852), and Moodie's *Roughing It in the Bush* (1852) and *Life in the Clearings* (1853). However, both women wrote until their deaths, placing them in the country for more than 50 years and certainly well past Confederation. Moreover, their books often dealt with survival and the rugged Canadian environment; these themes re-appear in other Canadian works, including Margaret Atwood's *Survival.* Moodie and Parr Traill's sister, Agnes Strickland, remained in England and wrote elegant royal biographies, creating a stark contrast between Canadian and English literatures.

However, one of the earliest "Canadian" writers virtually always included in Canadian literary anthologies is Thomas Chandler Haliburton (1796–1865), who died just two years before Canada's official birth. He is remembered for his comic character, Sam Slick, who appeared in *The Clockmaker* and other humorous works throughout Haliburton's life.

Arguably, the best-known living Canadian writer internationally (especially after the recent passing of Robertson Davies and Mordecai Richler) is Margaret Atwood, a prolific novelist, poet, and literary critic.

This group, along with Alice Munro, who has been called the best living writer of short stories in English, were the first to elevate Canadian Literature to the world stage. During the post-war decades only a handful of books of any literary merit were published each year in Canada, and Canadian literature was viewed as an appendage to British and American writing.

Much of what was produced dealt with extremely typical Canadiana such as the outdoors and animals, or events in Canadian history. A reaction against this tradition, poet Leonard Cohen's novel *Beautiful Losers* (1966), was labelled by one reviewer "the most revolting book ever written in Canada".

Canadian poet Leonard Cohen is perhaps best known as a folk singer and songwriter, with an international following.

Canadian Author Farley Mowat, best known for his work "Never Cry Wolf", also author of "Lost in the Barrens" (1956), Governor General's Award-winning children's book.

Criticism of Canadian Literature

Criticism of Canadian literature has focused on nationalistic and regional themes. Critics against such thematic criticism in Canadian literature, such as Frank Davey, have argued that a focus on theme diminishes the appreciation of complexity of the literature produced in the country, and creates the impression that Canadian literature is sociologically-oriented.

While Canadian literature, like the literature of every nation state, is influenced by its socio-political contexts, Canadian writers have produced a variety of genres. Influences on Canadian writers are broad, both geographically and historically.

Canada's dominant cultures were originally British and French, as well as aboriginal. After Prime Minister Trudeau's "Announcement of Implementation of Policy of Multiculturalism within Bilingual Framework," in 1971, Canada gradually became home to a more diverse population of readers and writers. The country's literature has been strongly influenced by international immigration, particularly in recent decades.

Canadian literature may be more difficult to discuss than most because of Canada's unique geographical and historical situation. Therefore, just as one piece of the Canadian social puzzle has often been, "is there a Canadian identity?," one recurrently important piece of the Canadian literature puzzle has been the question, "Is there a Canadian literature at all?"

This has been an ongoing point of debate since the mid-1800s, and is still being discussed in literary circles today. For example, a quick Internet search for university syllabi on Canadian literature courses will offer an overwhelming majority of professors who still discuss whether or not "Canadian" literature exists. For instance, one postmodern Can. lit. course offered as recently as 2002 at the College of William and Mary, Williamsburg, Virginia, includes this in the course syllabus: "The course starts off with a brief consideration of the 'problem' of Canadian identity: Is there such a thing? If so, what is it? And does that identity manifest itself in a national literature that is distinctly different from, say, British or U.S. literature? These are the sort of questions that get raised in Kroetsch's essays and Atwood's Surfacing."

In fact, it has frequently been suggested that the question, "what is a Canadian?" is entangled very intricately with the question "what is Canadian literature?" in a way that does not happen to so great an extent with other literatures. Leon Surette writes, "a disproportionate amount of commentary on Canadian writing has been cultural history (or prophecy) rather than truly literary commentary."

At the end of the debates, the verdict almost always returned is that there *is* a literature and an "identity" distinctly Canadian. However, because of its size and breadth, Canadian literature is often broken into sub-categories.

There are at least three ways that, traditionally, critics and scholars have chosen to deal with the geographic size and cultural breadth of Canadian literature. The most common, by far, is to divide it by region or province. There are anthologies of "Eastern Canadian literature" or "Prairie literature," for example. Another way has been to divide it by categorising the authors. For instance, the literature of Canadian women, Acadians, Aboriginal peoples in Canada, and Irish-Canadians have been anthologised as bodies of work. A third way has been to divide it by literary period, such as "Canadian postmoderns" or "Canadian Poets Between the Wars." Of course, as usual, Canadian literature is often studied in genre divisions as well, such as "poetry," "prose," "drama," and "criticism."

2

English-Canadian Literature

Writers have described Canada in many ways: for example, as a French or English colony, a "fifty-first state," a Pacific Rim country, an arctic giant, a friendly territory or an uninhabitable wilderness. Canadian literature has often had to deal with such differences in attitude, not just because many Canadian authors were born elsewhere and brought outsiders' expectations with them, but also because popular attitudes often perpetuated stereotypes of Canada. Three pervasive stereotypes portray Canada as a physical desert, a cultural wasteland and the raw land of investment opportunity. These distortions have created an audience for stereotypes, which Canadian writers sometimes reinforced by writing romantic adventures of the frozen North, in which everything local was savage or hostile and "civilization" was imported. But, over time, they sought to record local experience and to use literature to shape their own culture rather than to imitate or defer to the presumptions of another society.

A great literature presupposes an advanced and well-integrated society, a mature body and a self-conscious soul. The stirring records of explorers and pioneers, the cumulative chronicle provided in the journals of discoverers, in the memoirs of master-builders and in the pages of political and constitutional history, show clearly enough how the physical outline of Canada gradually took shape. By discovery and exploration, confederation agreements and purchase, the frontiers were ultimately set. The chronicle, if it were complete, should also tell of the parallel romance of industry, of commerce, of democratic government, of the Church, of education, art, and literature, for the great body, sprawling between two remote seas, and meandering northward into the Arctic sea, slowly became articulate. We speak of it as the voice of Canada, whether it be expressed in social custom, industrial enterprise, or individually in any other manner. Nationalism is a form of emotion which seeks adequate expression, and its most common and natural outlet is literature. A national literature, therefore, is one of the proudest and most potent symbols of separate national existence and ambition.

Canadian writers needed to be able to refer appropriately to local flora, fauna, place-names and events, and to use local vocabulary unapologetically. Words such as "moose" and "Medicine Hat," which once had been automatically comic because they transgressed English conventions of verbal propriety, became legitimate to use in literature. Native words ("igloo," "muskeg"), borrowings from French ("tuque," "gopher"), adaptations of English ("separate schools," "sky pilot"), regionalisms ("slough," "lakehead," "Bluenose") and vernacular cadences all became accepted during the 19th century. Still, the dominant vocabulary remained "international English," neither so highly localized as to impede communication nor different enough to require readers outside the culture to recognize the need to adjust to it. By the 20th century, the obliqueness of irony - a dominant literary mode - invited readers not to accept narrative literally or superficially, but to listen for more sophisticated implications. "Documentary", for example (a frequently used literary pattern), initially suggests that it conveys "truth."

But documentary takes several generic forms, from historical report and narrative sketch to drama and long poem, and the effect is more subjective than the word "documentary" implies: the glimpses of history that such works offer are also records of cultural and personal bias. In them, "history" is a fictional structure, a process of perceiving hierarchies of value and of constructing legends to encapsulate these values.

Many early long poems took narrative forms, making "history" a "story". More recent long poems - like another recurrent form, the story sequence, and like some novels and plays - are characteristically discontinuous in form. Often "metatextual," or self-referential, these works concern themselves with the language of literature and the processes of understanding as well as with empirical experience. Writer and reader consequently both become active agents in these literary works, interconnecting with the characters and the text.

The discontinuity, however, emphasizes the fragmentariness and the bias of understanding, often pointing to the existence of a "subtext" or alternative to the values of received traditions, values, or conventions.Several techniques have been used to imply the validity of various "marginal" stories, or regional, ethnic and sexual alternatives to conventional norms. Besides the discontinuous series, these include allegory, folktale, the fractured frame story, parodic humour and the ironic "embedded story" or *mise-en-scène.* Humour in Canadian literature appears more often in asides and understatement than in broad farce, and humourous writing often addresses serious subjects. Many writers became highly conscious that what distinguished them and their community was not the tale they told but the manner of telling it. By documenting local experience and using the local voice, they fostered regional and national culture. Newfoundland writers such as E.J. Pratt drew on a tall-tale tradition, Prairie writers such as Robert Kroetsch on an anecdotal tradition, and Ontario writers such as Margaret Atwood and Robertson Davies on a laconic interplay between irony and moral orderliness. Much of the force of their style derived from their control over regional cadence, which is as important as literal meaning because it reveals the inner motivations of the characters and also the social context. Narrative method is often indirect in Canadian writing (modes of parable and allegory are common); narrators usually hide their true feelings or have limited understanding of events around them, and the oblique or implied meanings are richer and more instructive than the obvious ones.

Legacy of Explorers

The dim beginnings of literature in many a nation are concerned with wanderings, quests, and pilgrimages of every sort. The literature of Canadian travel and exploration is rich in romance, but it rarely achieves literary excellence; being chiefly the work of adventurers from the British Isles, and elsewhere, it cannot always be described as Canadian. The total effect of these journals has not, however, been without literary significance. The old days were rich in character if not in literary finish, and these robust personalities have leavened in a strange manner the history and romance, the poetry and art of our day. Five years after Champlain founded Quebec, Captain Button spent the winter at the mouth of the Nelson river, in Hudson bay.

The names of hardy mariners, Hudson, Frobisher, Davis, Button, Fox, James, Baffin and many more, are bestowed upon bays, straits, islands and rivers in the north and west. Radisson and Groseilliers (1668) made a journey which resulted in the founding of the Hudson Bay Company (1670). The remarkable series of journals begins with that of Henry Kelsey, the boy adventurer, who set out, in 1690, from Fort Nelson. His narrative was printed in the *Hudson's Bay Report* of 1749. Then followed Alexander Mackenzie, who apologized for the lack of style in his work, but who reached both the Arctic and the Pacific, in 1789 and 1793.

The journal of Alexander Henry the elder, published in New York, was a work of shrewd observation, combining interest and charm. Samuel Hearne kept a journal which had much of his own vigour and dash. Its style was autobiographical, a method adopted by his successors, and it had the added zest of a virile defence of the Hudson 's Bay Company. This, together with his valuable data, and the thrill of many exploits, made the work a kind of best seller, passing through many English and foreign editions. Alexander Henry the younger, David Thompson, George Heriot, Cook, Vancouver, Franklin, these and many others have left their journals, some important and some of no value. Special mention must be made of Daniel W. Harmon, whose record of nearly two decades among the trading-posts on the prairies is a valuable document in social history.

Paul Kane's *Wanderings of an artist among the Indians of North America* (1859) and George Catlin's *The North American Indians* are chronological records of first-rate importance. Alexander Ross began a new era in frontier history. He wrote entertainingly, mingling plain fact and adventure in a curious jumble, yet in a style convincing and effective. From these we pass to a much later period and to another manner. J. W. Tyrrell, Henry Youle Hind, Sir W. F. Butler, Stefansson, these and others recorded their travels and discoveries with increasing skill. On the other hand, a new group of writers explored pioneer social life. In eastern Canada the *Diary of Mrs. Simcoe* left a memorable record of frontier days in Ontario.

John Howison visited Canada in 1819-20, and was followed by Anna Jameson, who spent the year 1837-8 in Upper Canada. Sir R. H. Bonnycastle lived in Upper Canada for some years and was an officer in the Rebellion. His two books are still useful. The list might be continued at a great length; but two books deserve perhaps special mention, *Ocean to ocean* by George Munro Grant, and *The search for the western sea* by Lawrence J. Burpee. Grant drew a vivid picture of Canada 's great inheritance, and Burpee traced be multiplying quests for the Pacific by land and sea.

Motifs and Patterns

Some commentators have interpreted literary indirectness politically and psychologically, finding in it a sign of national insecurity and a group feeling of inferiority. Others argue that indirectness is a healthy demonstration of the culture's ability to adapt an inherited tongue to its own purposes. Although the national character is not always the subject of literature, the culture's social attitudes and values can be seen in the language and forms it uses. Several specific narrative patterns recur in Canadian writing (1) a community walls itself off from the wilderness (the "garrison mentality"); (2) a person leaves the homeland, adjusts to the new world, then finds the "homeland" to be "alien"; (3) a person born in Canada feels like a permanent stranger in his or her own home; (4) people arrive in the new home only to find that they are excluded from power; (5) a person attempts to recover from the past the secret or suppressed life of a previous generation; (6) a woman struggles to come to terms with her own creativity and the inhibitions of her cultural upbringing (often told as conflict between colony and empire); (7) an apparently passive observer, surrounded by articulate tricksters and raconteurs, turns out to be able to tell both their story and his own, often ironically; (8) an adventurer turns failure into a form of grace; (9) a child grows up to inherit a world of promise, or a world of loss, or usually both at once; (10) a subjective historian meditates on place and memory; (11) a character celebrates space and wilderness, usually after a struggle to learn to accept that the wilderness provides spiritual therapy only on its own terms.To epitomize the character of their society, many writers have portrayed historical figures, such as Samuel Hearne, Louis Riel, Susanna Moodie, Sir John A. Macdonald, Emily Carr and William Lyon Mackenzie, each possessing a vision, but still an ordinary, less than heroic, frail human being. Settings often possess a symbolic dimension.

Catholic Québec recurrently figures as a land of mystery, attractive but enthralling and morally dangerous; Ontario as an enigmatic blend of moral uprightness and moral evasiveness; Atlantic Canada as a repository of old values; the North as a land of vision; the Prairies as a land of isolation and acquisition; and the West Coast as a dream of the future in which people often mistakenly believe. Europe often appears as the home of refinement and discrimination, the US as a land of crass achievement and tangible success, and Africa as the embodiment of all that seems "other" to Protestant rationalism. The land itself is recurrently associated with power, whether as property, region, a hostile force, the site of communication, a godly gift, the contested territory of competing cultural claims, the border, or the ecological medium in which human life integrates with all other living beings in Nature.

Although most Canadians live in cities, until recently writers used rural and small-town settings more frequently than urban ones, and they often ignored problems of class, race and poverty. From early on, however, writers such as Frances Brooke, Susanna Moodie, Sara Jeannette Duncan and Nellie Mcclung have been important analysts of Canadian political life. Often they sharply pointed out social divisions within Canada that male adventure writers ignored or underplayed. "Regional" writing also conveyed political stances, for by rejecting a single definition of "Canada," it asserted the viability of a nation with a plural character. Increasingly, moreover, native writers and writers who draw on ethnic backgrounds other than western European ones have examined the social limitations and political opportunities of Canadian pluralism.

The Colonial Writers

1760-1850

The Puritan and Loyalist Tradition.

Following the conquest, New England settlers, chiefly Puritan, emigrated in increasing numbers to Nova Scotia. Their social customs and political views were both native to their vigorous Congregationalism. School and church kept the faith vigorous; it coloured the institutions of the province, and inspired such literature as there was long after the great Loyalist influx. When John Howe emigrated from Boston, in 1776, taking with him the *News Letter* (re-established in Halifax under the name the *Halifax Gazette,* he founded the oldest newspaper in America, and also paved the way for a native literature. It was the *Novascotian,* founded in 1824, in which his son really established a native literary tradition, aiding it still further by the founding of the *Acadian Magazine,* in which his "Melville Island" shared honours with Oliver Goldsmith's *The rising village.* It was in such periodicals as these, and the *Quebec Magazine* (1791-4), the *Literary Garland* (1838-51) and others, that the first tentative literary efforts of Canada found their audience. The. Maritimes were constantly stirred by sectarian and political controversy. The pamphleteers among the Puritan clergy, and the robust lyrical patriotism and satirical outpourings of the Loyalists, were characteristic of all similar propaganda, and their work can scarcely be called literature. Many of the

Congregational clergy were trained in Harvard and elsewhere, and among the laity there were members of distinguished New England families, their social and intellectual training likewise impeccable. The Loyalist influx was rich in intellectual endowment, and the times encouraged clear-cut views on most issues. The issues at stake apparently called for forceful argument, at times bordering on invective, rather than the urbane, leisurely composition which one usually associates with art. On the whole the literature of the period was derivative, imitative, and inconsequential. Had the individualism of the Rev. Henry Alline found an echo in the imaginative writers, a national literature would have been born a century sooner that it actually was. Had Jacob Bailey found a cure for his nostalgia for the Old Colonies, or had Jonathan Odell loved Tory England not less but Canada more, both autobiography and poetry would have benefited. As it was, sectarianism founded three colleges, while patriotism worked out a constitution, established a militia, built towns, tilled the soil, launched ships, set up shop, and held its head high. Such literature as was required existed in the English classics; if one wished to try one's hand, there was Pope and Dryden, Goldsmith and Byron, Addison and Steele worthy of emulation, both as to thought and style.

First Hints of a Native Literature

The early Puritans, and later the Loyalists, however, came to establish homes and mend their fortunes. Largely from the New England states, English political, religious, social, and artistic customs and traditions, modified and individualized, came with them. The Revolution turned their gaze temporarily toward Great Britain, but they has been born in America, and their roots were in the soil of the New World. Judges, statesmen, preachers, teachers, farmers, and artisans were compelled to leave literature and art, those golden fruits of leisure, to another generation. With few exceptions in all the Canadas, books were written by transients.

It is the fashion to speak of Anna Jameson's *Winter studies and summer rambles,* Mrs. Frances Brooke's *The history of Emily Montague,* and similar works, as Canadian "classics". They are interesting as frontier chronicles, travel diaries, or settlement sketches, but certainly they are not Canadian: Oliver Goldsmith's *The rising village* (1825, 1836) has the distinction of being the first book of verse of a Canadian by birth to be published in Canada, and he shares honours with Thomas Chandler Haliburton in being the first to have a book published both in Great Britain and Canada. Goldsmith left no follower, although at the time he was popular. His influence on Canadian literature has been nil. The same can be said for Charles Heavysege, sometimes spoken of as the first Canadian dramatist.

The author of *Saul* (1859), a drama, *Jeptha's daughter* (1865), and other works in prose and verse, went to the Bible for his ideas, and to Shakespeare and Milton for his style. Even the praise of Hawthorne and Longfellow have not preserved him from oblivion, which, *Jeptha's daughter* excluded, he no doubt merits. What is true of Heavysege is also true of a long line of émigré poets, both Irish and Scots-Evan McColl, Alexander McLachlan, the "Canadian Burns", Nicholas Flood Davin, Thomas D'Arcy McGee, and many more. Only a lyric here and there survives in anthologies, of all those scores of books. The fact remains that national boundaries had been set, and that common dangers had decided the matter of separate national existence. Native sons were shortly to appear, heirs of great sacrifices and hardship, and of noble traditions as well, possessed of a passionate love for their country, and with leisure to paint and write of what they saw and felt. If James McCarrol survives in only two poems, they are "Canadian". If McGee is forgotten save for "Jaques Cartier", that will be remembered. Hints were not few that a national self-conscious literature was in the making. The form was borrowed from the masters, but the soul was increasingly Canadian.

Confederation Group

1850-1870

The Poets

W. F. Hawley published *Quebec, The Harp, and other poems* in 1829. "The Harp" won the medal of the Society for the Encouragement of Arts and Sciences, Quebec. Defying "everlasting Grumblers," he set down his poems for his own amusement, and the sources of his enjoyment were the beauties of the Canadian scene. The following year, also from the office of the Montreal *Gazette,* appeared *The Huron chief,* by Adam Kidd. The author writes from his own experiences among the Indians, and confesses his debt to Byron and Moore. Having tried the poem on the aborigines, he now flaunts the critics, as did Hawley, and records his observations for his own amusement, using Hawley's phrase. The first volume of verse published in Upper Canada, *Hamilton and other poems* (1840) was by William A. Stevens, collector. of customs at Owen Sound. His epic in four books invoking Homer, begins with the "mountain," goes back to Ararat and the Deluge, picks up Fulton and his steam-boat, returns to the "mountain" now Parnassus, and ultimately brings up at the jail, with a parting glance at the scenery. William Kirby likewise imitates Byron in a long loyalist epic poem, *The U.E.* (1859), in XII cantos, in which the heroism of Loyalist men and the pulchritude of Loyalist women are rehearsed in solemn dullness. These three books have only an antiquarian interest, perhaps, but they show how, for a quarter of a century, poets were essaying longer and more ambitious flights. They found publishers and readers, and in time successors more equal to the demands of art and the theme.

The first Canadian poet to strike nearest the national heart was Charles Sangster. Confederation was still far off, but the idea of political union had been tried out, and a wider scheme was in the offing assured by the growth of economic cohesion, and a spiritual cross-fertilization. While writing for the *Kingston Whig,* Sangster gathered together his fugitive pieces and published the *St. Lawrence and the Saguenay, and other poems* (1856). He was immediately hailed as "the National Poet of Canada".

In spite of the obvious influence of Wordsworth, Byron, and Tennyson, he discovered the Canadian scene and made it nobly lyrical. Twelve years later, Charles Mair published *Dreamland and other poems,* augmenting Sangster's lone national voice. Furthermore, it was Mair's *Tecumseh* (1886) that definitely announced a national drama. Building James M. Le Moine's historical essays into his knowledge of the West, just as William Kirby _and Gilbert Parker plundered Le Moine's *Maple leaves,* to enrich their

(Quebec romances, Mair proved that Canadian character and incident were suitable material for a native drama. He and Sangster had shown to such critics as Oliver Wendell Holmes, and to many in Canada, that the beauty of the Canadian landscape and seascape were worthy of exalted song.

Sangster and Mair were Canadians, but the noblest voice, the one with the widest range, that augmented the Confederation period, was an Irishwoman, Isabella Valancy Crawford. When she was eight years old, her family settled at Lakefield, Ontario, a district made famous by the Strickland sisters, and she became Canadian in every sense of the term.

After publishing a great many poems in the Toronto papers over a long period of years, her first collection, *Old Spookses' Pass and Malcolm's Katie* (1884), won the approval of Lord Dufferin. Her *Collected poems* (1905) reveal a rich mind, swift understanding of character, unusual powers of description, and a lyrical skill of high order, which place her among the real makers of Canadian literature. In strange contrast to Miss Crawford is George Frederick Cameron. whose chief distinction lies in his passionate championship of freedom. *Lyrics on freedom, love and death* (1887) contains too much violent protest, but his best poems are poignant and lyrical. Cameron searched out the downtrodden at the ends of the earth, and took leave, artistically, of his native land.

The Novelists

The Canadian school was ushered in with the Group of the Sixties. Within two or three years of each other there were born those who firmly established Canadian literature and rose to eminence in its various branches. Each, however, worked in a field prepared for him by his predecessors. *Roughing it in the bush* by Mrs. Moodie, by a strange freak of fortune elevated to a "classic", is a forerunner of our present-day frontier novels and plays.

The historical romances of Kirby and Parker are indebted to Mrs. Rosanna Eleanor Leprohon, one of the able contributors, along with Charles Heavysege, the Strickland sisters and others, to the *Literary Garland*. Her last and best novel *Antoinette de Mirecourt: or Secret marrying and secret sorrowing; a Canadian tale* (1864), a sequel to *The manor house of de Villerai*, successfully explored the romance, manners, and customs of the old régime. Hollowing this success, and perhaps influenced by it, appeared William Kirby whose novel *The golden dog* (1877) immediately took first place as a Canadian novel, a place which has not been seriously challenged up to the present. Kirby found his first impulse in the historic sites of Quebec itself, and the two stories woven into his romance are derived from the *Maple leaves* of Sir James M. Le Moine.

It is a sympathetic story, rich in characterization, and of literary worth. Anachronisms and historical blunders do not seriously impair the excellence of this book. Kirby and his most competent successors have worked in the field of historical romance.

Frances Brooke, wife of the garrison chaplain at Quebec, friend of Dr. Johnson,. Garrick, and other notables, has left, in *The history of Emily Montague* (3 vols., 1769), the best series of vignettes of social life in Quebec just subsequent to the conquest which we possess. This novel is modelled on Samuel Richardson's *Pamela*, and is therefore true to the early imitation by all Canadian writers of Old Country models. It was the first novel written in Canada,. but cannot be called a Canadian work.

Passing over *St. Ursula's convent, or the nun of Canada* (1824), by Julia Catherine Beckwith, the first novel by a.birthright Canadian, and of no literary value, we come to Major John Richardson. It is interesting to note that the year of his birth coincides with that of Haliburton and Mrs. Beckwith. As the author of *The War of* 1812, he became the first scientific historian of Canada, and his novel of the Pontiac conspiracy, *Wacousta, or the Prophecy* (1832), entitles him to the distinction of being the father of Canadian fiction. It is reminiscent of Cooper's *Leatherstocking tales.* Much of it is incoherent, melodramatic, and improbable, but it may still be read with enjoyment. The materials which he built into his novels, histories, and memoirs were gathered at first hand.

As we have seen, during the Confederation period a new life was taking shape, and a new, self-conscious art was in the process of making. It was not until 1880, however, that a singer appeared whose voice gave complete and satisfying utterance to the spirit of the new nation. In other fields the tendencies which had emerged now became fresh and substantial achievements. It was the' first time Canadians could say that they had a literature expressive of their character and ideals, faithfully reflecting the national spirit as well as the national *milieu.*

The Canadian School

1870-1900

The Group of the Sixties

Canada was now apparently ripe for a new

development in letters if ever she was to reveal any artistic significance. The Victorian age had deposited its greatest work.

The romantic movement in literature, modified by new classical influences, reflecting free and intensive inquiry in religion and science, and aided by the general diffusion of education, offered a democratic appeal in anticipation of the gradual rise of democracy. Longfellow, Whittier, Whitman, and Holmes lingered on in the United States, memorials to a vanishing tradition. Flaubert, Maupassant, Zola, Daudet, Renan, and Taine survived in France; Strauss in Germany, Mazzini in Italy, Turgeniev, Tolstoy and Dostoevsky in Russia.

The giants were not all dead. But it was to England, the England of the living giants, Tennyson, Browning, Rossetti, Swinburne, Thompson, Reade, Trollope, De Morgan, and George Eliot, that Canada was chiefly indebted, as it turned the year 1870. Scott and Dumas still ruled Canada 's novelists from their tombs, but this lingering coterie of poets echoed again and again in the descriptive poetry of the period just dawning, the sensuousness of the phrasing, and the self-conscious artistry.

Challenged by the new freedom in form and thought as well as by the witchery of the music, Canadian poets built upon the Victorian tradition. Retaining the general artistic and moral ideals of Great Britain, they betrothed these to distinctly national emotions and aspirations, with what result we shall see. Canada having attained the political structure of a Dominion, a rising tide of nationalism was inevitable. Material progress contributed to a profound sense of self-sufficiency, affecting the new nation in many ways. The poet and novelist, followed by the artist, became the legitimate interpreters of the awakened national consciousness. For the first time, therefore, was it possible to speak of a Canadian school of letters, which by an interesting coincidence, began in both English and French at practically the same moment.

Sir Charles G. D. Roberts (1860-) was a kinsman of Ralph Waldo Emerson. It was natural that his earlier work should be reminiscent of Milton, Keats, Shelley, Arnold, Tennyson, and Wordsworth. Canadian history was hardly taught in Canadian schools, and, of course, it is presumed that there was no such thing as Canadian literature. But George R. Parkin made the classics throb with vitality, and when he chanced upon a new voice, say Swinburne, his delight knew no bounds. He literally raced to his students, among them the group of cousins, Carman, Roberts, and the Strattons, that he 'might share the new-found treasure. Roberts had his poems published in the *Atlantic Monthly* before he was out of his 'teens, and his first book *Orion and other poems* (1880) was published when he was scarcely twenty.

This book is the corner-stone of the new literature of the Dominion. While it is reminiscent of his poetic masters, no borrowed grace of Arnold or sonorous phrase of Swinburne could disguise his originality. In *Avel* (1892) he reached his supreme moment, yet *In divers tones* (1886), *The book of the native* (1896), and, perhaps most of all, in *Songs of the common day* (1893), he consolidated and established his right to the title of "Father of Canadian poetry." Other books of verse followed, novels, nature stories, histories, translations, and so on, placing Roberts, for his very fecundity and versatility, as well as for his authentic artistry, upon the topmost round.

William Wilfred Campbell, though born in Ontario, published his first book *Lake lyrics and other poems* (1889) from his rectory in St. Stephen, N.B., thus augmenting the Maritime contribution. This book was reminiscent of the landscape round his old home near Georgian bay. *The dread voyage* (1893), *Beyond the hills of dream* (1899), and *Sagas of vaster Britain (1914)* established his position in the Group of the Sixties. He was a singer of real beauty when fully inspired. Over-conscious of his moral mission, and never forgetful of his British citizenship, his work tends toward the average in the Victorian tradition, but in a number of lyrics, such as "Indian Summer", "The Earth Spirit", "Bereavement of the Fields", and others, he achieved real distinction. It was as a dramatist, in *Mordred and Hildebrand* (1903) and *Poetical tragedies* (1908), that he made his greatest claim as a poet of power. Two novels and two historical works qualify him to approach the varied attainment of Roberts.

Bliss Carman inherited the same training and backgrounds as did Roberts, but he also inherited Roberts, derived encouragement from his success, and stimulation from his companionship. *Orion* kindled Archibald Lampman, then a student in Toronto, and Lampman fired the latent genius of Duncan Campbell Scott, and so on the impulse went. Carman came into his own with *Low tide on Grand Pry* (1893), and stepped at once, though comparatively late, into the front rank of American singers. His collaboration with Richard Hovey, in *Songs from Vagabondia* (1894), made the names of both famous as the nucleus of a group in American poetry demanding less conformity to old themes and patterns. This phase had its echoes in succeeding *Vagabondia* volumes, but Carman had really outgrown it when he issued *Behind the arras: A book of the unseen* (1895). From then on he reveals his pre-occupation with things of the spirit, and his life as well as his art became a long and not unsuccessful *Vestigia*. His collected *Poems* (1904), in two magnificent volumes, signalled his definite arrival. These contain the five books of *The pipes of Pan* (1902-4) and other groups of poems. Anyone desiring to understand his work will require the definitive edition of *The pipes of Pan, Sappho, One hundred lyrics* (1904), *Later poems* (1921), and *Ballads and lyrics* (1923). These last two are made up of several collections of verse appearing previously. Carman was a lyric poet of supreme felicity. If he sang too much he rarely sang ill. His insistent quest was the moated grange of the spirit, and whether it was a ballad of the sea, a song of Shamballah, an impressionist poem on April weather, or a.hymn to the pageantry of autumn, he "listened in", as he called it, for the voices of the Over Lord. The proof that his quest was not a failure may be had in many poems, and in the beauty and charm of his own personality.

Archibald Lampman has sometimes been called " Canada 's nature poet" and "the poet's poet"; he is also the people's poet. W. D. Howells welcomed his first book, Among *the millet* (1888), noting his "intimate friendship with nature" and "the right word upon his lips". *Lyrics of earth* (1893) and *Alcyone* (1899, 12 copies only) continued the theme, but with a persuasiveness and freshness quite new in Canadian literature. Within the circumscribed limits of his short life, confining employment in the civil service, and lack of any wide range of experience, he nevertheless found a world of endless enchantment and appeal. Master of colour and cadence, he stopped short of the sensuous phrasing of Keats and the pre-Raphaelite impressionism then in vogue. Maintaining a high artistry, consistent with his austere tastes, he ever looked beneath the phenomena of nature for hidden meanings. He was left unmoved by a rhetorical rhyme as much as by loud patriotism. Possessing urbanity and good taste, an immaculate ear for cadence, and a disciplined robust imagination, Lampman gave superb expression to his ideas of beauty and humanity. Duncan Campbell Scott edited a definitive edition of his poems in 1900.

Frederick George Scott (1861-), from the appearance of his first book *The soul's quest and other poems* (1888), and even *Collected poems* (1910), has multiplied his vigorous and sonorous lines without cessation. A churchman, and a Great War padre (C.M.G., D.S.O.), universally beloved, his verse abounds in moral and spiritual ideas, in warm humanity and fervent patriotism. Archdeacon Scott will be longest remembered for such lyrics as "The Unnamed Lake", in which are blended the inspiration of his beloved Laurentian country and a passionate quest for spiritual certainty.

Duncan Campbell Scott (1862-) won this encomium from Marjorie Pickthall: "He seems to me to have done some of the best Canadian poetry purely and naturally so-that has ever been done. Such things as his 'Half-Breed Girl' and `Night Burial in the Forest ' will one day stand very *high I* am sure." Time has proven the truth of that prophecy. Amid the onerous duties of the deputy superintendent-general of Indian affairs, he found time to write poems, plays, and short stories, which adorn Canada 's literature. *The magic house* (1893), *Labour and the angel* (1898), *New world lyrics and ballads* (1905), and other collections and plays culminated with his *Complete poems* in 1926. *The green cloister* appeared in 1935. No Canadian has surpassed his short stories, *In the village of Viger* (1896), and no single poem has surpassed "The Piper of Aril", which won the unstinted praise of John Masefield. Scott is a supreme technician. His work is rich in ideas, in swift spiritual insight, in colouring and cadence, and often in ecstasy and sheer magic.

Pauline Johnson, "Tekahionwake", Canada's first native-born woman poet, was, rightfully enough, a daughter of the head chief of the Six Nations. Her mother was a kinswoman of W. D. Howells. Nurtured on Byron and Scott, she moulded her verse on traditional lines. While on a visit to England her readings commanded great interest, and Gilbert Parker was able to secure a publisher for her first book, *White wampum* (1894). Following up the success of London, she toured Canada and the United States, publishing her next book, *Canadian born,* in 1903. A happy meeting with Chief Joe Capilano in London, and a further acquaintance in Vancouver, led to her *Legends of Vancouver* (1911), a book *which has* had a phenomenal sale. She collected her poems *in Flint, and Feather* (1912), and in the second edition Theodore Watts-Dunton added an introduction. Two books for boys on Indian themes, *The moccasin maker* (1913) and *Shagannappi* (1913), have had slight success. Pauline Johnson was a natural singer. Her themes run the gamut from poignant poems on her wronged people to swinging patriotic lines, from songs with Imperialism for their refrain to a mellow world embracing humanity. However, she is at her best when, in colourful and passionate phrase, blending pathos and humour, she sings of her race. In her the inarticulate ages of her forbears become vocal, and in so certain a manner that a half-dozen of her poems have found a lasting place in the golden book of Canadian song.

Haliburton had challenged the world with his Sam Slick series, and found publishers in Canada, the United States, and Great Britain. Richardson, in a smaller way, achieved the same distinction. It was not until Kirby's *Golden Dog* that any Canadian writer duplicated this success, and then only in the United States. Roberts's world success came in time,. but it was Sir Gilbert Parker who repeated the success of Haliburton and Richardson. Parker began as a poet, his greatest popular successes being songs *which* literally were sung round the world. With *Pierre and his people* (1892), he began his well-known books on the Canadian scene, working over the half-breed territory. When Valmond came *to Pontiac* (1895), a striking association of the Napoleonic legend with Canadian history, signalled his arrival, but it was *The seats of the mighty* (1895), following Kirby only in the period, which added a continual best-seller to his Canadian répertoire. Kirby was interested in character, Parker in the story simply.

Using the data gathered upon his world trips, many of them associated with his duties as member for eighteen years in the Mother of Parliaments, he wrote, among other books, *The battle of the strong* (1898), *The weavers* (1907), and *The judgment house* (1913), which carry the reader round the Empire, and have no doubt contributed to imperial solidarity. *The power and the glory* (1926) took the romantic story of La Salle as its theme. Parker's novels possess strong ethical and religious elements. They are distinctly romantic, and reveal no hint of psychoanalysis or other modern tendencies in fiction. He tells a story for itself, and tells it well.

The New Century

1900-1935

Senior Writers

We come next to the writers of the new century, who carried on the traditions of the Canadian school founded by the Group of the Sixties. Agnes Maule Machar created a name as "Fidelis", though it was but temporary. William Douw Lighthall (1857-) is known best by his novels, chief of which is *The master of life.* He has a collection of poems to his credit, *Old Measures* (1922). Both of these reflect his interest in Indian lore and the French régime. His brochures and pamphlets on philosophical and related themes are numerous.

Charles W. Gordon, "Ralph Connor" (1860-) would seem to belong to the group of the sixties, but his best work, commencing with *Black Rock* (1898), appeared almost at the close of the century. He has continued until the present, including *The man from Glengarry, The prospector, The foreigner, The major,* and many more, each epitomizing his experiences as a youth in Glengarry, his days as a missionary on the frontier, chaplain days in the Great War, and so on. He is interested in the story *per se,* and the moral which it illustrates. S. Francis Harrison, "Seranus", was a capable liaison writer. *Pine, rose,and fleur-de-lis* (1889), a book of poems, and *The forest of Bourg-Marie* (1900), a novel, strengthened the *bonne entente* with considerable artistry. Marshall Saunders is known to the world as the author of the children's classic *Beautiful Joe.* *My pets,* a sequel, *Bonnie Prince Fetlar, Jimmie Gold Coast,* and *Golden dickey* complete her chronicle of birds and furry friends. Her novels include *Esther de Warren.* Thomas Guthrie Marquis was one of the most fecund and useful writers. His editorial work on *Canada and its provinces, The chronicles of Canada, The makers of Canada,* and other series was monumental. The number of his critical and historical articles and brochures number scores. His novel *Marguerite de Roberval* (1899) goes back to the days of Cartier, a fine piece of work, which should be reprinted.

The best story for boys and girls written by a Canadian is *The king's wish* (1924), which shares honours with Miss Saunders's *Beautiful Joe* of being one of two books by Canadians printed in Braille for the blind. Marquis wrote verse, which possesses substance and lyrical skill. William Henry Drummond, born in Ireland, came to Canada when a boy and resided in Quebec. *The habitant and other poems* (1897) established his reputation as the poet of Quebec peasant life and character. He repeated this success in *Johnny Courteau* (1901), *The voyageur* (1908), and other works, his poems being collected in 1912.

While Fréchette welcomed him as "the pathfinder of a new land of song", later French critics have not shared the same enthusiasm. His *patois is* declared untrue, giving an erroneous idea of people who speak the traditional tongue of France. The kindly, human, and warm affection of Drummond's poems, however, have made the habitant widely known and loved. Theodore Harding Rand wrote little, but *At Minas basin* (1897) contains his best work. E. W. Thomson is remembered for his *Old man Savarin* selection of short stories, chiefly French-Canadian in theme; his poems are published in *The many-mansioned* house. The next important name is that of Ethelwyn Wetherald, for many years an editor of the *Ladies' Home Journal.* She collaborated with G. Mercer Adam in a novel entitled *An Algonquin maiden,* but it is as a poet that she will be remembered. *The house of the trees* (1895), *Tangled in stars* (1902), *The radiant road* (1904), *The last robin* (1907), *Tree top morning* (1921), and *Lyrics and sonnets* (1931), these are her principal collections, and they reveal a radiant spirit. Her lyrics are finely wrought, and are distinguished by delicate cadence and imaginative grace.

New Voices: The Poets

The later writers of the New Century have been numerous. We shall consider the poets first. Albert Durrant Watson began his literary career late, and with two volumes of essays on moral and spiritual themes. His first book of verse, *Wing of the wild bird* (1908), was a tentative effort, while his second, *Love and the universe* (1913), represents his best work. This was followed by several other volumes, and his collected poems in 1923. His poem "O Canada" is printed in many anthologies and church hymneries. Watson was a true cosmopolitan, and possessed a mind that Carman spoke of as ripe. Intensely inquisitive of all forms of belief, he was essentially a mystic. Such truth as he discerned spiritually he expressed in his song, and he has left a few poems worthy of remembrance, "Beauty Everywhere", "The Crow", "Goethe", and others. Helena Coleman's *Songs and Sonnets* (1906) and *Marching Men* (1917) reveal an ear for quiet cadences, such as in "Indian Summer" and "More Lovely Grows the Earth". Arthur W. H. Eaton (1849-) has been a prolific writer on history, legend, and genealogy. Of his three books of verse the chief is *Acadian ballads* (1905); "The Phantom Light of the

Baie des Chaleurs", and "I Watch the Ships", are popular poems. A. S. Smythe (1861-) is an eclectic philosopher with a sound poetical equipment. His best collection is *The garden of the sun* (1923). Annie Charlotte Dalton, though born in England, is perhaps Canada's greatest living woman poet. Her books are *The marriage of music (1910), Flame and adventure* (1924), *Christmas carols* (1925), *The ear trumpet* (1926), *The silent zone* (1926, *The amber riders* (1929), and *Lilies and leopards* (1935). Mrs Dalton possesses an unusually fertile mind. Her poems are packed with thought, amazingly varied, and variously beautiful. She commands the conservative measure with skill and achieves excellent effects in the free forms. Tom MacInnes (1867-) began with *Lonesome Bar* (1909) and *In amber lands* (1910); these were followed by *The rhymes of a rounder* (1913), each reflecting his vagabondage on the West coast, in the Yukon, and in the Orient. His *Complete poems* (1923) ensure his permanent place in Canadian literature. He is a poet of great originality and daring, singing with the lusty abandon of a Villon. *Chinook days is* a prose work, containing memories of the west coast days, and *The old boy is* a presentation of Oriental teaching. The collected *Poems* of Jean Blewett (1922), and the *Complete poems* (1930) of Isabel Ecclestone Mackay are especially rich in their humour and humanity. J. D. Logan is remembered for his literary criticism and many privately printed booklets of verse, beginning with Christian pantheism and ending with devout Catholicism expressed in sonorous and often beautiful fashion. Robert W. Service (1876-), the poet of the Yukon, drew a circle round that area, its physical characteristics and varied humanity, and made his microcosmos real in a swinging, somewhat vulgarized Kiplingesque style. *Ballads of a cheechako* (1907) and *Songs of a sourdough* are his best books. A collected edition of his five books appeared in 1930. He has written several romantic novels of the south seas and elsewhere. Florence Randal Livesay in *Songs of Ukrainia* (1915), translations, and *Shepherd's purse* (1923) has done work of rare beauty. John McCrea is best known for "In Flanders Fields", the title poem of the book by that name (1918). This was the best poem of the Great War, and is approached in quality by others less well known in his collection.

Frank Oliver Call (1878-) has published three books of verse, the best being *Blue homespun* (1925), in which he sings the beauties of habitant life. *The spell of French Canada* (1926) and *The spell of Acadia* (1928) are beautiful guide books to Quebec and Nova Scotia. Mrs. John W. Garvin, "Katherine Hale", published two chapbooks before her chief work appeared, *Morning in the west* (1923). This book reveals a poet of colour and cadence, with ability to handle new forms in a capable manner. Her most mature work is to be found in *The island and other poems* (1934). She is best known, perhaps through *Legends of the St. Lawrence* (1925), *Canadian cities of romance* (1922), and *Canadian houses of romance* (1926).

Arthur Stringer (1874-) is a poet first and a novelist second. *Watchers of the twilight* (1894) was followed by four collections which consolidated his-position. His latest work, *Out of Erin* (1930), and *Dark sail* (1933), stimulates the hope that he will yet turn exclusively to poetry, his first love. Of his novels, the prairie trilogy, *Prairie wife* (1916), *Prairie mother* (1919), and *Prairie child,* (1921) seems to us his best work.

Wilson MacDonald (1880-) has published seven books of verse, *The song of the prairie land* (1918), *The miracle song of Jesus* (1921; 1923), *Out of the wilderness*

(1926), *Ode on the diamond jubilee of Confederation* (1927), *Caw-Caw ballads* (1930), a book of satirical poems, *Paul Marchand* (1933), and *The song of the undertow* (1935). MacDonald sings of love and humanity, of social and religious protest, at times with whimsicality, at others with trenchant satire, now in lyrical cadences, and again in robust phrase. There are many strings to his lyre. Some of his shorter lyrics approach perfection.

E. J. Pratt (1883-) became known as an outstanding poet when his first book, *Newfoundland verse* (1923), appeared. It contains some of the best sea songs written by a Canadian. *The witches' brew* (1925) and *The titans* (1926) are long narrative poems in the objective manner, the former a hilarious extravaganza. *The iron door* (1927) deals with the problem of immortality and is Pratt's greatest poem. *Verses of the sea* (1930) is a selection of his sea poems. *The Roosevelt and the Antinoe* (1930) records superbly the epic of a celebrated rescue at sea; *The Titanic* (1935) is a significant poem on the sea tragedy. *Many moods* (1932) is Pratt's most satisfying collection. Pratt is one of the most vigorous and original poets of the modern group.

Marjorie Pickthall, born in England, came to Canada when six years old. When but sixteen, she won a poetry prize with "Song of the Nixies", and her progress from then on was rapid and certain. Her first book, *Drift of pinions* (1914), already revealed a poet of golden maturity, unsurpassed by any first offering in Canada. *Little hearts* (1916), a novel, appeared while she was in England during the War, and was followed by *The lamp of poor souls* (1917), a new collection of verse in which all the poems of her first book were reprinted. Upon her return to Canada, *The bridge* (1921), a novel, was published, and *The woodcarver's wife,* a collection of poems, chiefest of which was the one-act play, the title piece, of unsurpassed excellence. *Little songs* (1925) appeared posthumously, and a first collection of short stories, *Angel shoes* (1923). *Complete poems* (1927) give Marjorie Pickthall a supreme place among Canadian poets. The light celestial quality of her drifting rhythm, the unblemished beauty of her jeweled vocabulary, the colourful magic of her descriptions, the haunting loveliness of her ideas, so often associated with the symbolism of the Church, these she lovingly shepherded into the fold of her undying song.

The following have to their credit one or more books and are representative of this period: Louise Morey Bowman, *Moonlight and common day* (1922) and *Dream tapestries* (1924); George Herbert Clarke, *The hasting day* (1930) and *Halt and parley and other poems* (1934); Archibald MacMechan, *Late harvest* (1934); James B. Dollard, Col *lected poems* (1920); Alfred Gordon, *Poems* (1916) and *Vimy Ridge* (1918); Dorothy Livesay, *Signpost* (1932); Norah Holland, *When half gods go* (1924); Lilian Leveridge, *Over the hills of home* (1918) and *A breath of the woods* (1926); Laura I;. *McCully, Mary Magdalene* (1914); Leo Kennedy, *The shrouding* (1934); Gertrude MacGregor Moffat, *A book of verse* (1924); Alan Creighton, *Earth call* (1936); Marian Osborne, *Poems* (1914), *The song of Israfel* (1913), and *Sappho and Phaon* (1926); Beatrice Redpath, *Drawn shutters* (1914) and *White lilac* (1919); Sara E. Carsley, *Alchemy* (1935). Arthur Bourinot gathered the best of his six books into *Selected poems* (1935). Lloyd Roberts has published *England over seas* (1914) and *Along the Ottawa* (1927), also *The book of Roberts* (1923), a delightful book of vignettes on his father, Carman, and the old King's College days. J. E. H. Macdonald's *West by East* (1933) appeared posthumously, and was illustrated with rare charm by his son Thoreau. A. M. Stephen published *The rosary of Pan* (1923), *Land of singing waters* (1927), *Brown earth and bunch grass* (1931), and *Vérendrye* (1935), an epic poem, together with two novels and two anthologies. Virna Sheard, besides *The miracle* (1913) and *The ballad of the quest* (1922), has written fiction. Watson Kirkconnell has published many translations and studies of European poets; his chief work is to be found in *The eternal quest* (1934), a poem in twelve parts, and supremely in *A Canadian headmaster* (1936),,a life of his father. Norman Gregor Guthrie, "John Crichton", began with *A vista* (1921), and this was succeeded by *Flower and flame* (1924), *Pillar* of *smoke* (1925), and *Flake and petal* (1928). These revealed a poet of the flowers and a fine artist. Passion predominates, sensuousness, perhaps, but refined.

His study of *Archibald Lampman* (1927) proved that the poet was also an able critic. Francis Sherman published in 1896 his only book of poems, *Matins,* which was followed by little pamphlets of verse privately printed for his friends-In *memorabilia mortis* (1896), *A prelude* (1897), *The deserted city* (1899), and *A Canadian calendar: XII lyrics* (1900). Louise Imogen Guiney called him "a shy shepherd from Canada", whose *Matins* were "very misty and fawn-coloured and Rosettian."

Pre-Raphaelite he was and mystical, but his poetry is strong and beautiful and all compact of thought. Like Phillips Stewart *(Poems,* 1887), Sherman deserves better recognition. Theodore Goodridge Roberts, a prolific writer of novels and short stories, published a collected edition of his poems, *The leather bottle,* in 1934. His work is rich in romance, in humanity, and in full-throated music. Cecil Francis Lloyd first became known as an essayist of rare insight and charm. Several volumes of verse, privately printed, were sifted for his collected poems, *Landfall* (1935). Pelham Edgar, who first sponsored Marjorie Pickthall, also discovered Audrey Alexander Brown. *A dryad in Nanaimo* (1931) marked the advent of a new poet, limited in range yet exquisitely beautiful in such poems as "Laodamia". *The new provinces* (1936) is a collection by six poets of the new tradition; read together with Nathaniel A. Benson's anthology, *Modern Canadian poetry* (1930), and *Our Canadian literature* (1935), an anthology by Bliss Carman and Lorne Pierce, they give some idea respecting the progress of poetry in Canada.

New Voices: The Novelists

Some of the best fiction produced in Canada has been in the short story form, and in this Duncan Campbell Scott and Marjorie Pickthall are outstanding. *Canadian short stories,* selected by Raymond Knister, provides a good anthology of our most representative work, while the introduction and bibliography enable the reader to find his way through the forest of productions in recent years.

In the novel our chief work has been done along historical and regional lines. This seems natural in a large country, rich in material, requiring spokesmen for its widely separated and distinct types and areas of national interest It was a far cry from *The trail of* '98 by Robert W. Service, one of the popular first successes in Canadian regionalist fiction, to *Anne of Green Gables* and *Anne of Avonlea,* by L. M. Montgomery, or *Duncan Polite,* by Marian Keith. Since then the work in this genre has been growing in importance. Mrs. Nellie McClung's stories of western life and character, *Sowing seeds in Danny* (1908), etc., and *Janey Canuck in the west* (1910) by Mrs. Emily Murphy, were surpassed by Mrs. Laura Goodman Salverson's *The viking heart* and *Lord of the silver dragon,* revealing the pioneer spirit of the Viking breed. Mrs. Isabel Mackay's *The window gazer is* a somewhat melodramatic idyll linking east and west.

Norman Duncan has made memorable the life of the Newfoundland and Labrador fishermen in *Battle royal, Down north, Billy Topsail,* and *Doctor Luke of the Labrador.* Robert Stead has written several novels with prairie backgrounds; *Neighbours* (1922), *The smoking flax* (1924) and *Grain* (1927), especially, are well constructed and true to life. Frederick Philip Grove followed up his ventures in the essay form with his best prairie novel, *Settlers of the marsh* (1926), and a fine autobiographical novel, *A search for America* (1927). *Our daily bread* (1929) is almost morbidly dark and depressing. *Yoke of life* (1930) stands second among his novels.

Robert Watson's *My brave and gallant gentleman, Gordon of the lost lagoon,* and other melodramatic stories of the west and far north, have had some success here and abroad. Theodore Goodridge Roberts has been voluminous in the short story and fiction. *The wasp* and *The red feathers* (1906) are his best works. James Le Rossignol has done good work in re-interpreting French life and lore in *jean Baptiste,* a novel, and *The flying canoe,* a book of legends. Mabel Dunham's *The trail of Conestoga,* a story of Mennonite settlement; *The men of Kildonan,* by J. H. McCulloch, a stirring romance of the Selkirk settlers; the *Jalna* novels, by Mazo de la Roche, with her earlier romances, *Explorers of the dawn* (1922), *Delight* (1926), and especially *Possession* (1923), have witnessed the growing quality of Canadian fiction. Canadian novelists - are slowly acquiring skill in their craft, their chief need being a more profound character analysis, in which Grove, Callaghan, and Mazo de la Roche offer excellent promise. Pierre Coalfleet's Solo (1924) and *Hare and tortoise* (1925) combine maturity of thought and originality of style. Morley Callaghan's stark realism and trenchant style are prophetic of a new development of the novel in Canada. His early work leaned too heavily upon hiss models, especially Hemingway, but with growing independence, ripeness, and artistry, his latest novels, *Such is my beloved* (1934) and *They shall inherit the earth* (1935), prove that he has arrived. So far, however, the few novels which are apt to live are traditional in style, and associated with historical and regional themes. It seems certain that immediate progress will be still in these fields, keeping pace with a lively exploration of Canadian archives by the new generation of historians.

Drama

Mention has already been made of the dramatical works of Charles Heavysege and Charles Mair. Mair initiated the Canadian tradition. Parker's first and greatest success was an adaptation of *Faust*. Campbell also turned from the Canadian scene in *Mordred and Hildebrand. Daulac is* his only Canadian theme. Duncan Campbell Scott's *Pierre* is an idyll of Quebec, full of humour and tender sympathy. Robert Norwood has given us *The witch of Endor* (1916) and *The man of Kerioth* (1919), a tragedy of Judas Iscariot. The best Canadian dramatic work has been in the one-act play. Marjorie Pickthall's poetic tragedy *The woodcarver's wife* was successfully produced in Montreal and Toronto, and is the best of its kind, Out of the Montreal Little

Theatre movement grew the collection of nineteen plays in *One act plays* published by the Canadian Authors Association, Montreal Branch. Vincent Massey edited two significant collections of *Canadian plays from Hart House,* which contain much good work by Denison, Scott, Osborne, Mackay, Aikins, and others. *The unheroic north* (1923) by Merrill Denison and *One third of a bill* (1925) by Fred Jacobs did as much for native drama as Tom Thomson's paintings did for Canadian art. *Six Canadian plays,* edited by H. A. Voaden (1930) are deliberately Canadian. They are in various keys, the sardonic and grim prevailing. This is due to the fact that settings are chosen quite remote from pastoral areas.

The hostile wilderness seems to attract Canada's young playwrights as it has the Group of Seven in art. However, Canada has many facets, and can accommodate a wide variety of artists. It is likely that no one novel or poem shall ever become *the* Canadian epic, any more than one canvas or marble may be crowned *the* Canadian masterpiece. The Dominion Drama Festival may correct two faults which have hitherto prevented outstanding drama in Canada,-an incompetent knowledge of the theatre, and a shallow understanding of human character.

The Essay

The essay in Canada began with a formal imitation of Addison and Steele. It was a vehicle for many practical motives. Howe's "essays" were speeches on all manner of themes. In the Maritimes the early essay exhorts and denounces, fathers religious and political controversy, and only in "The Club", instituted by Howe, did it become whimsical and partially detached. Goldwin

Smith was a pamphleteer and a polemicist, who wrote blithely on everything with insufficient information, but plenty of force. His work cannot be called Canadian. John Reade and George Stewart, both journalists, wrote literary reviews, somewhat uncritical, and passionately loyal to made-in Canada products. James Cappon of Queen's may be said to have laid the foundation of literary criticism in Canada with his studies of Roberts and Carman, two books which will remain standards for a long time.

Thomas O'Hagan, although a prolific poet, excels in the essay, marked by urbanity, cosmopolitan sympathy, whimsy, and the graces of style. His best work is *With staf and scrip* (1925). Bliss Carman wrote several series of essays, reviews, and comment for United States papers, before he published *The kinship of nature* (1904), *The friendship of art* (1904), *The poetry of life* (1905), and his favourite and best work, *The making of personality* (1908). Each collection is built around a thesis, but for all that the whimsical and discursive good talk entitles them to a place. *Brown waters and other sketches* (1915) and *In a fishing country* (1923), by W. H. Blake, are two books of rare beauty and charm.

MacMechan, poet, critic, and historian, has surpassed all others in the traditional essay form, *The poster of Bagdad and other fantasies* (1901), *The life of a little college* (1914), *The orchards of Ultima Thule* (1922), and his historical sketches of Maritime history, *Old province tales* (1924), *Sagas of the sea, There go the ships* (1929) and others, made him the unrivalled chronicler of his adopted East. Sir Andrew Macphail, besides history, criticism, and fiction, has done his best work in essay form. *Essays in Puritanism* (1905), *The book of sorrow* (1909), and *Essays in fallacy* (1910) reveal a vigorous mind. The total effect is one of delight and and happy surprise, merging the criticism of life and letters in informal and persuasive style. Sir William Osler was, like Macphail, also a medical knight, gifted with a rare mind and a style of classic beauty. Of his several volumes of essays, *Counsels and ideals* (1905) and *A way of life* (1914) are chief.

Cecil Francis Lloyd is the best known and most competent of the recent essayists. *Malvern essays* (1930) is a collection from leading Canadian periodicals. Ray Palmer Baker has written *A history of English-Canadian literature to the Confederation,* the best work on that period. J. D. Logan and MacMechan have also produced histories of Canadian literature, supplementary in many respects. V. R. Rhodenizer's *Handbook of Canadian literature* and *An outline of Canadian literature* by borne Pierce may also be mentioned.

William Arthur Deacon, in *Pens and pirates* (1923), *Poteen* (1926), etc., and in his weekly reviews has established his name as a vigorous, constructive, and piquant essayist and critic. Pelham Edgar has confined himself chiefly to the novel in his critical books, *The art of the novel* (1930) and a study of Henry James. His prefaces and reviews are of a high order, and have had a marked influence upon Canadian letters.

Nature Writers

Canada has pre-empted a unique place in the history of literature with the short story dealing with wild animal life. The dim beginning of this genre was in the animal sketches by Mrs. Traill, but it was Sir Charles G. D. Roberts who, became the undisputed laureate of the animal kingdom. His first book, *Earth's enigmas*

(1896), placed him at once at the front as originator and master, and he has never surpassed the stories in this collection. A list of his books in this field would fill much space, but *The kindred of the wild* (1902), *Kings in exile* (1910), and *Wisdom of the wilderness* (1922) may be taken as representatives of his best work. Ernest Thompson Seton (1860-) is more concerned with scientific observation.

Roberts simply aims to show that beasts and birds have an existence which is in many respects kindred to our own, and that we should sympathetically understand them. This he does with verbal artistry. Seton began as an artist and a scientist, and these elements are mixed in his work-Wild *animals I have known* (1898), *The tail of the sandhill stag* (1899), *The biography of a grizzly* (1900), and others. Seton is a closely observing scientist, Roberts writes from recollection; the former is an artist among animals, the latter a poet in the forest spaces. Seton's work belongs to science, Roberts's to imaginative literature.

Marshall Saunders in *Beautiful Joe* (1894), *My golden Dickie* (1916), *Bonnie Prince Fetter* (1919), *My pets* (1935), and succeeding books on bird and animal pets is a crusading humanitarian in the circle of domesticated animal life. W. A. Fraser in *Mooswa and others of the boundaries* (1900), *The outcasts* (1910), and *Thoroughbreds* (1902) shows a predilection for the race horse. Archie McKishnie (1878-) entered this field with *Love of the wild* (1910), and later wrote *Mates of the tangle* (1925), both vigorous and swiftly moving romances, less artistic than Roberts, and less informative than Seton.

A special group of nature writers may be called local colourists. Most of Canadian verse, and the best of Canadian essays perhaps, would come under such a head. However, the following will illustrate our meaning.

Arthur Heming (1870-) was first an artist, but was forced to write his first book, *The drama of the forests* (1921), when the author failed to produce the manuscript after he had provided the illustrations. He has followed this success with *Spirit lake* (1907) and *The living forest* (1925), books rich in forest lore by one who knows northern forests in all their aspects. Mrs. Traill's *Studies in plant life of Canada* (1885) and *Pearls and pebbles* (1894) belong to a different category, as does also her *Rambles in a Canadian forest* (1859). In the same class may be mentioned Mrs. Anna Jameson's *Winter studies and summer rambles* (1836), a favourite still.

There are also S. T. Wood's *Rambles of a Canadian naturalist* (1915), and Peter McArthur's farmstead essays *In pastures green* (1915), *Around home* (1925), and *Friendly acres* (1927). The farm chat by McArthur, the "Sage of Ekfrid", has not been equalled in Canada for quaintness, ripeness and charm. Several of MacMechan's essays, two books by Grove, *The turn of the year.* (1923) and *Over prairie trails* (1922), Mrs. Murphy's *Seeds of pine* (1914), and other similar works might, with equal justice, be included here.

The Hunourists

Canada has made a unique contribution also to the literature of humour, which has challenged the attention of the world. Roberts's nature stories have sold in larger quantities in Scandinavia, Germany, or Czecho-Slovakia than in Canada. Haliburton had a larger market in the United States or Great Britain, France or Germany, than at home. His *Sam Slick* (1836) therefore became an important event in the history of Canadian literature. He followed this success with many other books, but they never achieved the same hearty laughter. His politics, criticisms of United States republicanism, propaganda for British imperialism, satirical tirades against Durham and the Canadian Reformers, all this has ceased to be either funny or informing and is long since forgotten. Yét Sam Slick lives on, not the high priest of Toryism, but the lord of laughter, gibing at the Yankee and the Maritimers, playfully and without rancour.

James DeMille produced two score books, many of them for boys, which owe their impulse to Haliburton. *The Dodge Club* (1869) was a forerunner of Mark Twain's *Innocents abroad.* Twain includes him in his *Library of American humour.* George Thomas Lanigan wrote a book of *National ballads* (1865), in which appeared his well-known "The Ahkoond of Swat". He was an Irishman with an eye for absurdities, as may be seen in this book of verse and in his *Fables of G. Washington Esop* (18'78).

William Henry Drummond has been considered as a poet. He has created several humorous characters, Leetle Bateese, Johnnie Courteau, and other "Canayen" types which continue in popularity. Stephen Leacock (1869-) has carried on the Haliburton tradition in his humour of exaggeration. The best of his work is contained in *Literary lapses* (1910), *Sunshine sketches of.a little town* (1912), and supremely in *My discovery of England* (1922). His work has been uneven, due perhaps to the pressure of insistent editors and publishers, and we, are fortunate in having a selection of his best pieces, *Laugh with Leacock* (1930). He is a kindly critic of the foibles and absurdities of humanity.

He has created no outstanding character, being content to show up, with his ridiculous verbiage and boisterous fooling, the nonsense of common people about him. Sara Jeanette Duncan was a humorist of great ability. She gathered her observations upon many travels, and set them in such books as *A social departure* (1890), *Those delightful Americans* (1902), and *His royal happiness* (1914).

With the crispness of Jane Austen, a distinguished prose style, and an allpervading whimsicality, she has established her right to live in Canadian literature. Of Peter McArthur we have already spoken. *The red cow and her friends* (1919) and *The affable stranger* (1920) added little to his happy annals of the old farm. His book on Leacock is an excellent interpretation. There is a growing literature of caricature, but time only will tell how important it is. Canadian literature is, on the whole, too solemn. There is not nearly enough hearty laughter. More blythe and jocund, it will be closer to Canadian life. John W. Garvin, who did much for Canadian literature in his anthologies, did not live to see his last, *Cap and bells* (1936), through the press. This anthology of humorous verse may have a salutary influence.

Biographies

Endless biographies have been written in Canada, but few of them have risen above the level. The *Makers of Canada* produces but two or three good lives, such as *Haldimand* by Jean McIllwraith, and *Simcoe* by Duncan Campbell Scott. Biographers have been too partisan, either laudatory or hypercritical. This accounts for the inferiority of lives of George Brown, Macdonald, Laurier, and others. Mrs. O. D. Skelton's *Thomas*

D'Arcy McGee (1925) is a notable exception. Such men as D. B. Read did good service in collections of portraits of eminent men, but they were uncritical, and the resources of archives not available. There is much encouragement in several recent books, notably *Thomas Chandler Haliburton*, by V. L. O. Chittick (1924), Chester Martin's *Lord Selkirk's work in Canada* (1916), *Lord Durham by* Chester- New, (1929), which won the Empire gold medal, and *James Wolfe, Man and Soldier*, by W. T. Waugh.

Both George M. Wrong and J. L. Morison have written on *The Earl of Elgin*. Harvey Cushing's *Life of Sir William Osler* (1925), like Morison's, is the work of a scholar abroad. Biographies of Canadian writers are increasing in number and in value. Carl Y. Connor's *Archibald Lampman* (1929) is a work of combined biography and criticism. Lorne Pierce has written *Marjorie Pickthall: A book of remembrance*. (1924), and *William Kirby: The portrait of a Tory loyalist* (1929). *The Makers of Canadian Literature* contain at present twelve short biographies and critical estimates. Autobiography has not fared so well. Sir Richard Cartwright and Sir Charles Tupper both wrote their reminiscences, but they are largely apologies for their political activities.

Fifty years in Western Canada: The abridged memoirs of Father Morice (1930) is a valuable work supplementing the writing of Father Lacombe, the Rev. George McDougall, and others. *The high romance* (1918), by Michael Williams, is an intimate chronicle of his spiritual development, and in the same class as *A search for America*, by Frederick Philip Grove. Both look upon the world without as courageously and with as much discernment as they gaze upon the mind and heart within. Canadians are not given to calm self-analysis, and these two books, the first of any significance since Henry Alline's *Life and Journals* (1806), prompt the wish that there may be many more equally good. The general interest *in* biography and autobiography leads one to believe that Canadian literature will shortly overcome the handicap of weak character portrayal.

Historical Literature

Even to catalogue Canadian historical literature of importance would require many pages. Bibliographies, selected and classified, are easily accessible. The early work of Kingsford, Christie, and others may be dismissed as both unscientific and unreadable. Such historians as Smith and Dent were prejudiced. Haliburton remains as a curiosity; Bourinot is remembered chiefly for his *Parliamentary procedure.* Roberts, still the most readable of the short histories, is not up-to-date, and so on one might go.

Few Canadians approach Parkman. Richardson's *War of* 1812 has all the vigour of a first-hand account, and is not without the amenities of style. Agnes C. Laut, with the sense of news value and the literary facility of a journalist, has popularized the journals of explorers and pioneers. Her best work is *The conquest of the great northwest* (2 vols., 1908). George M. Wrong, the pioneer of the modern school of Canadian historians, combines well-balanced judgment and a persuasive style. He is a prolific historian, and has few equals as a stylist, as *The Earl of Elgin* (1908), *A Canadian manor and its seigneurs* (1908; 2nd ed. 1926), *The rise and fall of New France,* (2 vols., 1929), and *Canada and the American revolution* (1934) will prove. Archibald MacMechan has been considered under another head. While his books are composed of separate papers, he has gone to the original sources and writes with rare grace. H. A. Innis's *The fur-trade in Canada* (1927), Alfred L. Burt's *The old province of Quebec* (1933), and Chester Martin's *Lord Selkirk's work in Canada* (1910), are examples of the work of the new school.

Few historians have equalled the imaginative quality and the fluent and vivid style of William Wood's *The fight for Canada* (1904), In *the heart of old Canada* (1913), and similar works. The *French régime in Prince Edward Island* (1925) by D. C. Harvey is the most authoritative and readable of Maritime histories. J. S. McLennan's *Louisbourg* and J. C. Webster's *The forts of Chignecto* (1930) are excellent of their kind. The *war trail of Big Bear,* by W.-B. Cameron, is a first-hand and readable narrative. F. W. Howay has multiplied his publications on the history of the North West coast, on which he is a leading authority.

Sir Arthur Doughty combines precise knowledge of the sources and an attractive style in *The fortress of Quebec* (1904), *Quebec under two flags* (1903), *The siege of Quebec* (6 vols., 1901), and other books. The publications of the Champlain Society, the Canadian Historical Studies, and *The Canadian Historical Review* contain some of the most modern historical research. *The chronicles of Canada* and *Canada and its provinces* have been useful and deservedly popular. W. S. Wallace contributed two volumes to the *Chronicles,* edited the *Canadian Historical Review* for a time, edited some volumes in the Champlain Society publications, etc., and has many historical texts to his credit widely adopted in schools, besides *The dictionary of Canadian biography* (1925), and several popular works of a biographical nature. With the appearance of better writers, and abler as well as better equipped historians, the standard is constantly being raised. The supremacy of fiction is being challenged abroad by great works in biography and history as sources of enjoyment. No real advance can be made in Canada until the hidden wealth of the archives is explored to add substance, fresh colour, and new life to the nation's story, and the story of its master-builders.

3

French Canadian and Quebec Literature

The French régime did not give rise to any Canadian literature in the proper sense of the word. The books which at that period were written about Canada were by Frenchmen who, for the most part, had done little more than visit Canada; and their work was published in France. Among these works should be mentioned the *Récits de voyages* of Jacques Cartier, the discoverer of Canada, and those of Samuel de Champlain, the founder of Quebec; the *Histoire de la Nouvelle France* of Marc Lescarbot; the *Relations* and the *Journal* of the Jesuits, which are of importance both for the history of the Jesuit missions and for the general history of the colony of New France; the work of Father Lafitau on *Les moeurs des sauvages américains comparées aux moeurs des premiers temps,* and that of Father Charlevoix, on *L'histoire et description générale de la Nouvelle-France, avec le journal historique d'un voyage fait par ordre du roi dans l'Amérique septentrionale.*

Marie de l'Incarnation, the superior of the Ursulines in Quebec, who came to Canada in 1639, and who died in 1672, has left literary memorials of rare value, which describe the author's spiritual experiences, and which contain valuable observations on the period of Canadian history between 1639 and 1672. These works, and some others less important, constitute an introductory chapter to the history of French-Canadian literature. The first chapter really opens after 1760, under the British régime.

Period of Canadian Origins

1760-1860

Canadian literature in French was not destined to begin immediately after the cession -of Canada to Great Britain. The French Canadians, ruined by the Seven Years War, applied themselves at first to the work of economic reconstruction. They sought, indeed, by means of the school, to preserve the best traditions of French culture; but they found it difficult to devote themselves to work of a literary character.

Newspapers and Political Prose

It was in the newspaper and in the parliamentary struggles of political life that the first manifestations of literary life among the French Canadians were seen. The Constitutional Act of 1791, which created in Canada proper parliamentary institutions, gave rise also to political eloquence; and this was manifested in turn in the speeches in the Legislative Assembly and in the editorials of the newspapers. The orators of the Legislative Assembly have not left any important literary remains. They fought with determination and sometimes with real eloquence for the rights of the French language in parliament, and for the conquest of those parliamentary liberties necessary to the proper administration of public affairs. Among them, the most distinguished was Louis Joseph Papineau, who was speaker of the Legislative Assembly of Lower Canada from 1815 to 1837, and who was endowed with exceptional oratorical powers that gave him a great influence both in the Legislative Assembly and before popular audiences. Several of his speeches, which display an oratory more popular than academic, have been preserved in the newspapers of the time.

Political prose is represented especially at this time by the work of a great journalist named Etienne Parent. Parent became editor of the *Canadien* in 1822, at the age of twenty years. This newspaper having ceased publication in 1825, Parent, aided by some others, revived it in 1831, and he remained its director until 1842. The greater part of the contributions made by the *Canadien* toward the control of the purse by the Assembly, toward the reform of the Legislative Council, and toward responsible government, were due either to his pen or to his inspiration. His contemporaries regarded him with esteem both as a thinker and as a writer. These same qualities are seen in the addresses which he delivered after 1842 on questions relating to sociology and political economy. These addresses, which have been published, are assuredly one of the best contributions to the political and philosophical prose of the period.

The thought in them is solid, fecund, and often bold; and it is expressed in clear and vigorous language, sometimes heavy, but more often animated and adorned with flowers of speech and classical allusions. Among his best addresses may be cited the following: *Importance de l'étude de l'économie politique; Du prêtre et du spiritualisme dans leur rapport avec la société; Considérations sur notre système d'éducation populaire, sur l'éducation en général; L'Intelligence dons ses rapports avec la société;* and *Considérations sur le sort des classes ouvrières.*

History

It was during this period of the beginnings of French-Canadian literature that the first works on the history of Canada were published. The first, in point of date, of the French-Canadian historians was Michel Bibaud. His *Histoire du Canada* (3 vols., Montreal, 1837-8) covers the political history of Canada from the beginning to 1837. This work, in which the author takes as a rule the part of the *bureaucrates* against the French-Canadian *patriotes,* in the struggles to which the parliamentary régime of 1791-1837 gave rise, was not much appreciated by French-Canadian readers. Bibaud's *Histoire* was soon discredited, both because of its Tory sympathies and because of the lack of information from which a first essay in the field of Canadian history necessarily suffered.

While Michel Bibaud was publishing his work, another historian, Francois-Xavier Garneau was working on another *Histoire du Canada,* which began to appear in 1845. This work, which appeared in three volumes, was the fruit of patient researches made in Canada, France, and England; it was written in a style full of life, and, without being an apology for the French Canadians, it explained loyally their political attitude under the British régime, when they sought to control, through the voting of subsidies, the administration of the governor and his council. Garneau's *Histoire* covers the history of all the French colonies in North America from their beginnings up to the treaty of 1763, by which France ceded Canada to Great Britain; from that date, the author concentrates his narrative on Canada proper. Garneau deserves the credit of having written a work of such importance, so well documented, so rich in facts and ideas, at a time when the sources of Canadian history were so inaccessible, and the means of general culture were so insufficient. The work of Garneau was welcomed with enthusiasm; and the plaudits of the public were awarded to the worker who had wrought with so much science and art. The youth of French Canada were inspired by the story of Canada's past; and it would be difficult to exaggerate the influence of Garneau's *Histoire,* not only on contemporary politics, but also on the growth of French-Canadian literature. It became the chief authority for the facts of history, and also the book from which young writers, and especially young poets, drew their inspiration.

Poetry

During the period from 1760 to 1860, poetry appeared only in the form of timid attempts. It appeared in the newspapers, in the form of popular or military *chansons,* or in the form of odes or satires. The Revolutionary War and the War of 1812 gave rise to some poetry of a rather popular nature, in which the poetic art is somewhat naive, and is less notable than the historical interest which these first Canadian verses have. The best contributions in verse furnished to the newspapers of that day were by Joseph Mermet and Joseph Quesnel, two poets who came from France, the latter of whom was to remain and die in Canada. Michel Bibaud, while he was busying himself with history, was also attempting the practice of poetry. He composed satires, *chansons,* and epistles, in verse-forms somewhat ponderous; and it is he who deserves at least the credit of publishing the first collection of poems in French-Canadian literature, *Epitres, satires, chansons, épigrammes, et autres pièces de vers* (Montreal, 1830). Another historian, F. X. Garneau himself, combined the practice of poetry with that of history. Garneau's poems draw their inspiration from the author's historical and patriotic interests; and he may be considered the creator in French Canada of patriotic poetry, of the kind which Octave Crémazie was later to develop and adorn. Probably the most harmonious and adroit of the first French-Canadian poets - at least of those who belong to the period of literary origins — was Joseph Lenoir. He was endowed with a great lyric sensibility; he had the soul of a Lamartine; and he followed the masters of romantic poetry. He did not, however, rise to the full measure of his powers, for he was cut off by a premature death, at the age of thirty-nine years. His poems were gathered much later, and were published under the title of *Poèmes épars* (Montreal, 1916). It was under the dominating influence of Garneau's *Histoire du Canada* that French-Canadian poetry got into its stride.

The Second Period

1860-1900

This period is distinguished from the preceding by a sudden and more fruitful activity in the intellectual life of French Canada. The causes of this advance are diverse. First of all, there was the influence of Garneau's *Histoire du Canada,* to which reference has already been made. The reading of the *Histoire du Canada* developed among French Canadians the feeling of patriotism, pride in the past, and ambition for a better future — aspirations broader and more solid than had been entertained before. The desire arose to augment, by means of art and letters, the national patrimony of which Garneau had revealed in his work the unsuspected proportions. A poet arose at this moment, named Octave Crémazie, who, inspired by Garneau, injected into his songs a patriotic fervour which moved all his contemporaries. Crémazie and Garneau were the true originators of a new literature.

Octave Crémazie was a bookseller. It was in his bookshop at Quebec that gathered those who were destined to take part in the literary movement of 1860. Fortuitous circumstances brought together in Quebec a group of men who were passionately devoted to letters, wished to write, and made a joint effort to succeed. They were F. X. Garneau and Etienne Parent, the oldest of the group; Antoine Gérin-Lajoie, librarian of parliament, who had perforce come to Quebec, since parliament was sitting there; Joseph Charles Taché, director of *Le Courrier du Canada;* P. J. O. Chauveau, superintendent of public instruction; Hubert La Rue, a professor in Laval University; the Abbé J. B. A Ferland, also a professor at Laval, where he occupied with distinction the chair of Canadian history; and last, but not least, the young Abbé Raymond Casgrain, vicar of the cathedral at Quebec, enthusiastic and romantic, who had just published his first *Légende.* This young abbé was a fervent admirer of Garneau and of Crémazie; and he wished to see a true Canadian literature spring into being under the inspiration of a new enthusiasm — a literature abundant, artistic, better than the timid attempts that had preceded the work of Garneau and of Crémazie. All these men were wont to gather in the bookshop of Crémazie. They read there the latest books imported from France; they chatted there about their literary projects; and they sought ways and means of uniting their efforts in order to make them more fruitful. Thus it was that in 1861 they founded the first French-Canadian literary review, *Les soirées canadiennes,* and that the *Foyer canadien* was launched also in 1863. These literary periodicals made it possible for writers to publish their work, and to make themselves known to the public; they were also a standing invitation to writers to work and to produce. It was under the influence of these men and by their enthusiastic co-operation that a new literary movement arose which was destined to produce immediately happy results.

Poetry

Crémazie was in truth both the soul of the new group and the father of French-Canadian poetry, at any rate of that which was to give us the first durable work. This poetry was above all one of patriotic inspiration, impregnated through and through with contemporary ideas and prepossessions. It is, indeed, only by reason of the state of mind of Crémazie's compatriots that one can explain its character.

No other poetry, it would seem, could at that hour of Canadian historical development, take root and flourish. The poetry of that day joined with history to comfort souls disillusioned and anxious for the future, and to stimulate hope and ambition. Crémazie was the sounding-board of his contemporaries.

No poem shows this more clearly than that entitled *Vieux soldat canadien* or that entitled *Drapeau de Carillon*. It was his aim to make his country loved — its landscape, its legends, the customs of its inhabitants. The poems entitled *Le Canada, Les Milles Iles, Le chant des voyageurs,* and *La fiancée de Marion* are all inspired by this aim of the poet. At the time, Crémazie was fond of philosophical or moral themes. *Le poème des morts* is perhaps the most personal of his writings, and the most vigorous; one may couple with it the very realistic verses entitled *La promenade de trois morts.* He was too fond of reading the masters of French contemporary poetry not to reveal in his work some traces of the imitation of their work, and notably that of Victor Hugo; and he was unfortunate in that the exile to which he was condemned at the age of thirty-five years put an end to his literary career. Crémazie did not fulfill the promise of his early genius. But, short as was his career, and few as were his poems, he founded a school. It was the example and the work of Crémazie which gave birth to what one may call the school of patriotic poetry in Quebec; and the two chief disciples of Crémazie were Louis Fréchette and Pamphile Lemay.

Louis Fréchette published his first volume, *Mes loisirs,* at the age of twenty-six years. In it he confesses that his chief inspiration came from Crémazie, and from the desire to continue his work. Like Crémazie, he considered poetry the expression of the national life, and he devoted himself especially to singing the facts of history.

No doubt his first volumes, such as *Pèle-mêle, Fleurs boréales,* and *Les oiseaux de neige,* are composed of songs in which the author celebrates nature and the feelings of human life; but it is *La légende d'un peuple,* published in 1887, which appears to illustrate best the dominant inspiration of Fréchette's work. This work is a sort of heroic poem in which the author extracts from the history of Canada episodes which lend themselves to poetic treatment. The sequence of these poems comprises a sort of national history seen from the mountain-tops, and composed of the most significant events in Canadian life. *La légende d'un peuple* is an heroic poem at once lyrical and oratorical. Its eloquence commits the poet to the banality of the commonplaces of rhetoric; but many of its verses contain the best work of Louis Fréchette.

Pamphile Lemay was, like Fréchette, a disciple of Crémazie. But he devoted himself, more than Fréchette, to the intimate and calmer poetry of rural life and domestic life. He wrote also patriotic poetry, but in a different manner. He was the great ancestor of the French-Canadian poetry of the soil. He loves the fields, the hearth, the familiar customs and traditions, and he takes from them the habitual and most sincere theme of his work.

He does not fall into the epic and sometimes unnatural eloquence of Fréchette; he writes with sincere emotion; he composes, often in verses too careless, poems in which the trivial details of the countryside live again. His principal works were *Essais poétiques* (1865), *Les vengeances* (1875), a versified romance in which the author tells the story and paints the picture of the life of his people, *Une gerbe* (1879), *Fables canadiennes* (1882), *Petits poèmes* (1883), and *Les gouttelettes* (1904), which is a collection of sonnets, the first of the kind in French-Canadian literature, and one in which the author, more intent on his art, has best given the measure of his talent. He treated again in it a great number of subjects, drawn from Canadian life, which he had dealt with in his previous works.

After Louis Fréchette and Pamphile Lemay came William Chapman, who continued to exploit the patriotic theme. He was less happy than his two predecessors. He treated again great historical subjects, in which he imitated the eloquence of Fréchette, and he fell also, and more heavily, into the commonplaces of rhetoric. His oratorical poetry, in which moving strophes are found, was often applauded. His best work is to be found in his *Aspirations* (1904), *Les rayons du nord* (1910), and *Les fleurs de givre* (1912).

It was in this same period, in which Fréchette and Lemay were leading the choir of the Muses, that appeared the work of Adolphe Poisson, Alfred Garneau, and Appolinaire Gingras. Adolphe Poisson published *Heures perdues, Sous les pins,* and *Chants de soir,* in which he treated of patriotic and historical subjects, and in which he translated also into verse his deep emotions. Alfred Garneau ushered in a new type of poetry, in which the traditional theme of history gave place to the more intimate inspirations of the soul. His poems are psychological. The Abbé Appolinaire Gingras sings at once the customs of the countryside and his own sensibilities. He is fond also of excellent *badinage.* All these characteristics are found in his *Au foyer de mon presbytère* (1881).

History

Poetry, in French Canada, was born of history; but history was destined to develop, during the period 1860-1900, parallel with poetry. The Abbé J. B. A. Ferland, a professor at Laval University, followed Garneau in telling the story of the French régime in Canada. He gave a course of lectures at Laval University which were the occasion of these new studies; and he gave them with great rigour of method, correcting or making more precise the historical points which Garneau had not sufficiently elucidated. His *Cours d'histoire du Canada* was written in simple language, devoid of ornament, which yet held attention by means of its clarity and the sincerity of a style which betrayed neither the eloquence nor the emotion of Garneau. The Abbé Henri Raymond Casgrain, one of the most enthusiastic pioneers of the group of 1860, began by publishing some Canadian legends, such as *Le tableau de la Rivière Ouelle, Les pionniers canadiens,* and *La jongleuse;* and these legends led him to history. He had been too much influenced by the reading of F. X. Garneau not to wish to continue his work taking up certain phases of it with a view to digging deeper.

The Abbé Casgrain therefore devoted himself to the writing of monographs. These constitute some of the finest pages of Canadian history. Some of his principal works are the *Histoire de la Mère Marie de l'Incarnation,* the *Biographies canadiennes* (dealing with some contemporaries, such as Octave Crémazie, Philippe Aubert de Gaspé, and Antoine Gérin-Lajoie), the *Histoire de l'Hôtel-Dieu de Québec,* the *Pèlerinage au pays dEvangéline* (in which he studies the Acadian question), *Montcalm et Lévis* (in which is told the story of the British conquest), *Une seconde Acadie,* and *Les Sulpiciens et les prêtres des missions étrangères en Acadie.*

The last are written in language graver and more restrained than the first; but in all of them the historian reveals a vivid imagination. Occasionally his historical method yields to the exigencies of a feeling which determines his sympathies in too arbitrary a manner. To this same period belongs Gérin-Lajoie's *Dix ans d'histoire du Canada, 1840-1850,* which tells the story of the first ten years of politics under the union of the two Canadas, and in which the author brings before our eyes the conquest of responsible government by Baldwin and Lafontaine.

After these historians, or with them, others devoted themselves to the study of particular aspects of Canadian national life, and published numerous monographs. Joseph Edmond Roy made a specialty of *la petite histoire,* the history of customs and manners; and this is found in picturesque abundance in the five volumes of his *Histoire de la seigneurie de Lauzon.* He published also a considerable number of monographs, such as his *Souvenirs d'une classe au Séminaire de Québec.* All his works were written without much literary care, but with a pleasant simplicity, in which one sometimes misses nevertheless a more methodical art. Benjamin Sulte was the most indefatigable and most inquiring "researcher" of this period. His inquiries carried him into all sorts of questions, and in particular into the history of his native place, Three Rivers. He wrote with a good humour which made it difficult to criticize his work, and which was in turn its charm and its weakness.

Among his principal works were his *Histoire des Trois-Rivières,* his *Histoire des canadiens-français,* his *Mélanges d'histoire et de littérature,* his *Le coin de fées,* his *Chronique trifluvienne,* his *Pages d'histoire du Canada,* his *Histoire de la milice canadienne,* and *La bataille de Chateauguay.* Since his death his scattered writings have been republished under the title of *Mélanges historiques.* Narcisse Eutrope Dionne wrote, among a large number of other historical studies, the following: *Jacques Cartier, Samuel de Champlain, Pierre Bédard et ses fils,* and *Historique de Notre Dame des Victoires de Québec.* Laurent Olivier David combined politics and history, and among his works were *Les patriotes de 1837-1838, Biographies et portraits, L'union des deux Canadas,* and *L'histoire du Canada depuis la Confédération, 1867-1887.* Ernest Myrand brought to the writing of history both intellectual curiosity and imagination. He published

Une fête de Noël sous Jacques Cartier (which was an ingenious historical fiction), *Sir William Phips devant le Québec, Frontenac et ses amis,* and *Noëls anciens de la Nouvelle France.*

History having been a form of literature very much cultivated between 1860 and 1900, many other authors might be added to those named above authors of works of varying degrees of importance. We mention only Pascal Poirier, the author of *Origines des acadiens* and *Le Père Lefebvre et l'Acadie,* Mgr. Lionel Lindsay, the author of *Notre Dame de la Jeune Lorette en la Nouvelle France,* and Ernest Gagnon, the author of *Le Fort et le Chateau Saint-Louis* and *Louis Jolliet.*

Fiction

During this period of the origins of Canadian literature, the novel drew benefit from the enthusiasm roused by history and poetry. It was on history, or the life of the people, with their customs and their heroic sufferings, that the literature of the novel was first built. Philippe Aubert de Gaspé published in 1863 *Les anciens canadiens,* a novel of manners in which were recounted some of the great episodes of Canadian history, the scenes of the campaign of 1759 which ended in the battle of the Plains of Abraham. This novel had a great success.

Readers recognized in it a faithful picture of Canadian life at the period when this life was being transformed under the new influence of the British conquest. They liked to find in it a description of customs and traditions which they felt ought to be preserved; and the style of the novel, which partakes of the character of a natural and picturesque conversation, contributed in itself to render more popular the tales and legends which are the basis of the novel. At the same time as *Les anciens canadiens* was appearing, Antoine Gérin-Lajoie published *J ean Rivard.* This novel was at once a novel of manners and a social document. It told the story of a young colonist who had exchanged college for the forest and rhetoric for the culture of the soil. It reminded the youth of French Canada of their duty to resist the wave of emigration which was sweeping them toward the industries of the United States, and to attach themselves to the land. Despite a style which is a little forbidding, this book, which was full of rustic life and descriptions of popular customs, obtained a great success. In 1865 another author, Napoléon Bourassa, published yet another novel, the subject of which was borrowed from the painful history of the dispersion of the Acadians by the British government. *Jacques et Marie* had the success due to a story of Acadian heroism; but its execution was somewhat uneven.

The historical novel was popular with readers of this period. Joseph Marmette took advantage of this popular taste to publish a series of novels in which the characters and events of Canadian history live again. The principal works of this romancer are *François de Bienville, L'intendant Bigot,* and *Le chevalier de Mornac;* but these works are of unequal value. Laure Conan also attempted the historical novel; and, with a more artistic pen, she wrote *A l'oeuvre et à l'épreuve, L'oublié,* and *La sève immortetle.* Her *Angeline de Montbrun* was a successful pioneer in the field of the psychological novel. There was published in this period hardly more than one novel of adventure. This was *Une de perdue et deux de trouvées* (2 vols., Montreal, 1874), by Georges Boucher de Boucherville (1814-1898).

Chroniques, Essays, and Oratory

The literature of legends, *chroniques,* and popular tales was one of the most abundant toward the end of the nineteenth century in Canada. It was a product of the renaissance of 1860. The Abbé Casgrain, in publishing his *Légendes,* had himself set the example, and those who worked with him followed in his footsteps. Joseph Charles Taché published *Trois légendes* and the picturesque tales entitled *Forestiers et voyageurs.* Hubert La Rue published studies of Canadian popular and historical *chansons,* and narratives of *Un voyage autour de l'Ile d'Orléans and Un voyage sentimental sur la rue Saint-Jean.* Later P. J. O. Chauveau wrote *Souvenirs et légendes.* He was also the author of a study of *François-Xavier Garneau, sa vie et ses oeuvres,* and he was destined to achieve by means of his academic speeches the reputation of an orator.

Faucher de St. Maurice was one of the most voluminous authors of this period, and published numerous books of travel, such as *De Quebec à Mexico, A la brunante, Choses et autres, De tribord à babord,* and *En route.* Hector Fabre, who was a journalist, has left a volume of *Chroniques;* and Napoléon Legendre collected his *chroniques* in two volumes entitled *Echoes de Quebec.* But the most brilliant writer of *chroniques* in this period was Arthur Buies. He contributed to journals and gathered in numerous volumes articles in which he embodied the fruits of his social and geographical studies. Among the chief of these were the following: *Chroniques; Humeurs et caprices; Chroniques, voyages; Petites chroniques pour 1877; L'Ouatouais supérieur; Au portique des Laurentides;* and *Récits de voyage.* In his pages are to be found intelligence, sensibility, and originality. Adolphe

Routhier was one of the most highly appreciated writers and speakers of his day. His works, which were fairly numerous, comprise critical and literary studies, books of travel, novels, and speeches. His easy prose, naturally charged with feeling and fancy, was highly esteemed by contemporary readers. His chief works were *Causeries du dimanche, Portraits et pastels, A travers l'Europe, De Québec à Victoria, Québec et Lévis, De l'homme d Dieu, Conférences et discours,* and a novel entitled *Le centurion.* Lastly, one must add to this group the name of an orator who shone above all others in his parliamentary eloquence, Sir Wilfrid Laurier.

Period of Literary Renaissance

1900-1930

With the beginning of the twentieth century there appeared clear signs of intellectual and literary progress among the people of French Canada. Writers became more numerous and more artistic; and the public, more prone to read Canadian books, has thus shown a more sympathetic attitude, in this renaissance of French-Canadian letters. French-Canadian literature has in this period penetrated deeper into the life of French Canada; it has aroused more intellectual curiosity; and it has called for a higher art in those who write. On the other hand, the people of French Canada have appeared more anxious to create for themselves a literature which should be at once an illustration of the genius of their race and a safeguard of its best traditions, menaced by an intrusive cosmopolitanism. The Société du Parler Français au Canada, founded at Laval University in 1902, has contributed, through its studies of French-Canadian speech, to the creation and development of a literature which should take as its objective everything which might preserve the popular speech, the manners and traditions of rural life.

For twenty years it was the centre of an activity which conferred on literature great benefit. In addition, in the dying years of the nineteenth century, there was formed in Montreal about 1895 an *École Littéraire,* somewhat more exclusive, in which met several poets who had the desire and the ambition to revivify a Canadian poetry which had exhausted itself in its lyrical efforts in history and patriotism. It turned to the secrets of the soul, to the study of conscience. This was the inspiration of the new poetry.

Literary criticism, born in the first years of the new century, contributed also to stimulate writers, and to attract to the Canadian book a favour which it had lacked. If criticism does not create either talent or genius, it calls forth at least useful efforts, and by giving more publicity to the work of writers, it creates an intellectual atmosphere more propitious for the development of literature.

Poetry

The form of literature which was the first to benefit by the renaissance of 1900 was poetry. The *École Littéraire of Montreal* produced the first works which bear the marks of a new inspiration, one more personal and more careful to achieve original artistic forms. Charles Gill was a member of this school, which had its headquarters in the Château de Ramezay. He dreamed of an heroic and lyric poem of nature, of which the river St. Lawrence should be the center — that vast river so grandly picturesque, so full of history and legend. The design was admirable; but the poet had not the time to execute it. He succeeded in sketching only one book of this epic, the uncompleted *Le Cap Eternité.* In it the author rejoiced in the bold and unequal flights of his epic inspiration. Emile Nelligan is still the most appealing of the poets of the *École Littéraire.* His misfortunes as well as his poems have elicited for him the favour of the public.

At the early age of twenty years his mind was darkened by insanity. He had foreseen this disaster of his inner life, and had foretold it in the most touching of his poems, *Le vaisseau d'or.* His poetry spouted forth in the fever of his thought and imagination; it is full of the anxieties and sorrows of the poet; and it is couched in verses which are not all above reproach, but which reveal in general a new feeling for artistic form. Albert Lozeau had, like Nelligan, a tragic fate. It was his bodily health that was too soon shattered. Condemned by illness and infirmity to a painful seclusion, he consecrated the leisure of his isolation to study and to poetry.

He sang of his *Ame solitaire,* and published *Le miroir des jours, Lauriers, and Feuilles d'érable.* He took up in turn all the lyric themes-first of all, love, of which he dreamed in his bedroom, then solitude, the vanity of things, religious feeling, and sometimes the world of nature, in which he had revelled in the first years of his youth, but which he was scarcely destined to see again save through the windows of his room. His poetry is as a rule sincere and full of feeling, sometimes uneven, but most often captivating. Gonzalve Desaulniers (1863-1934) confined the wide field of his poetry to nature. *Les bois qui chantent* is characteristic of his romantic and dreamy inspiration, of the need he felt to listen not only to the melancholy murmur of the trees, but also to that of the shore and the sea.

Jean Charbonneau belongs also to the *École Littéraire,* of which he was one of the founders. He delights in philosophical poetry; but he does not always bring to it the clear vision of a strong and precise mind. His flight often is through the clouds. His chief works are *Les blessures, L'âge de sang, Les prédestinées,* and *La flamme ardente.* Albert Ferland is less ambitious than Jean Charbonneau. He has made himself above all the poet of the woods and the forests. Under the general title *Le Canada chanté,* he has published *Les horizons, Le terroir,* and *L'âme des bois.*

The poetry of the soil, which was born of the movement called forth by the studies of the Société du Parler Français au Canada, has provided some of the best work of our times. Nérée Beauchemin, who had written before 1900 his *Floraisons matutinales,* refined and perfected his regionalist inspiration in the collection of poems entitled *Patrie intime,* which he published at the end of his life. In it he sings of the Canadian landscape, the parish bell, the French race from which he sprang. Mme.

Blanche Lamontagne is a poet who has developed most fully the theme of the soil. She has published, without perhaps seeking often enough a new inspiration, many volumes, in which she reveals a delicate feeling and a filial worship of that Gaspesian country which owes to her some of the best poems it has inspired. Her best works are *Visions gaspésiennes, Par nos champs et nos rives, La vieille maison,* and *Ma Gaspésie.* Lionel Léveillé, who signs himself "Englebert Gallèze", loves also to sing of rustic life. His work is lacking in inspiration, but it combines, with great precision of detail, a vivid picture of things and people. He has published *Les chemins de l'âme, La claire fontaine, Chante, rossignol, chante,* and *Vers la lumière.* Alphonse Désilets and Hector Deniers, the first in *La brise du terroir,* and the second in *Les voix champêtres,* have also contributed to bring to the attention of the public the picturesque life of their own people.

While the poets of the soil are celebrating the work and the customs of the countryside, others appear oblivious to these themes, but seek their inspiration in foreign countries, or shut themselves up with their own thoughts, or concern themselves almost exclusively with the forms of their art. Paul Morin is the most artistic of these searchers after rare beauty. In his *Paon d'émail* he has painted colourful landscapes, scenes of Greek life; he delights in the exotic, and in experimenting with rich and sonorous forms of poetry. His *Poêmes de cendre et d'or* are marked by the same characteristics and contain some of his finest verses. Guy Delahaye has attempted symbolic poetry in his *Phases,* and René Chopin has shown, first in his *Coeur en exil,* and later in his *Dominantes,* the care he takes to clothe his dreams and his meditations in well-chosen rhythms, cadences, and artistic forms.

Outside these groups, which are formed about a similar object or a similar preconception of art, there are numerous poets who, attached to no school of poetry, have freely practiced all kinds of poetry or developed all the themes of poetry. Alphonse Beauregard has written a philosophical poem in *Les forces et les alternances.* Jules Tremblay wrote short moral, philosophical, or patriotic pieces in *Des mots, des vers, Du crépuscule aux aubes, Les ferments, Arômes du terroir,* and *Les ailes qui montent.* Louis Joseph Doucet has published a number of volumes in which he has treated, without sufficient artistic grace, all the themes and sentiments of lyric poetry. The Abbé Arthur Lacasse has filled his *Heures solitaires,* his *L'Envoi des heures,* and his *Les heures sereines* with the expression of religious sentiments and with recollections of rural and domestic life. Religious sentiments — those of the inner life — have been treated more deeply and more artistically by Lucien Rainier (the Abbé J. N. Melançon) in *Avec ma vie.* Lucien Rainier draws his inspiration from his own meditations and from a rather original view of the phenomena of the conscience. His art is most delicate.

Two poets of to-day have struck again the lyric note in French-Canadian verse, Robert Choquette and Alfred Des Rockers. Robert Choquette is endowed with a vigorous imagination, which leads him to express his thought and his feeling in figures of speech often bold and original. *A travers les vents* was a remarkable effort, though of uneven merit, written when the author was twenty years of age. *Les nouvelles poésies* reveals a firmer thought, presented in more ambitious forms, which are sometimes akin to epic poetry, as in his *Metropolitan Museum.* Alfred Des Rockers has taken up the theme of the poetry of the soil, but he treats it with a more robust preciseness, with a realism at once more exact and more crude. He mingles with it, however, a lyric quality that transforms into powerful verse the poetry of little things. He has shown the vigorous force of his talent in *L'offrande aux vierges folles* and A *l'ombre de l'Orford.*

One must add to all these lyric poets the names of some poetesses who resemble them in the form of their art, but who are distinguished from them by their too great preoccupation with the theme of love and passion. These are Alice Lemieux, Simone Routhier, Jovette-Alice Bernier, and Eva Sénécal.

Émile Coderre, who had previously devoted his efforts, in his *Signes sur le sable,* to describing the poetry of popular manners, has inaugurated a new genre of poetry in popular language, in his volume entitled *Quand j'parle tout seul.* He writes under the pseudonym "Jean Narrache"; and he paints in his verses realistic pictures of human wretchedness, which he contrasts with the pride and luxury of the rich.

A Franco-American poet who lives in the United States, Rosaire Dion, belongs quite naturally to the Canadian group. He writes a lyric poetry in which, as in his *Les oasis,* he pays increasing attention to colour and artistic form.

History

Canadian history does not cease to call forth new studies. The sources of information are now fuller and more accessible, and investigators are making use of these new means of research in order to pursue further the study of the past. During the last thirty years, two historians in particular have produced much work of a high grade, Thomas Chapais and the Abbé Lionel Groulx. Thomas Chapais began with researches into the French colonial régime, and by publishing two authoritative monographs, *Jean Talon* and *Le Marquis de Montcalm.* As professor of history at Laval University in Quebec, he has given a course of historical lectures on the British régime in Canada, in which over a series of years he has studied British colonial policy in Canada. These lectures form a most objective picture, marked by a balanced judgment, of the political life of Canada from 1760 to 1867, the date of Confederation. This course of lectures forms eight volumes, fully documented. The Abbé Lionel Groulx, professor at the University of Montreal, has also brought his inquiries to bear on the French régime and on the British régime. His chief books are *La naissance d'une race, Lendemains de conquête, Vers l'émancipation, La Confédération canadienne, L'enseignement français au Canada,* and *La découverte du Canada.* In these are exhibited the dominant qualities of the author, his careful research, his patriotic feeling, his desire to revive by his works all the pride of the French-Canadian race.

Beside these two principal historians, one must mention Alfred De Celles, who succeeded especially in popularizing history in his books on *Papineau,* on *Lafontaine et son temps,* and on *Cartier et son temps;* and the Abbé Auguste Gosselin, who wrote the history of the French-Canadian Church in the form of numerous episcopal biographies, beginning with that of Laval, the first bishop of Quebec. The Rev. Henri Arthur Scott wrote *L'histoire de Notre Dame de Foy,* only the first part of which was finished, and some studies on *Nos anciens historiographes.* Mgr. Amédée Gosselin is the author of a valuable and well-documented work on *L'instruction du Canada sous le régime français.* The Abbé Ivanhoë Caron has told *L'histoire de la colonisation de la province de Québec;* and the Abbé Olivier Maurault, in his *Marges d'histoire* and in *La paroisse,* writes of the historical and artistic life of Montreal. Gustave Lanctôt has done a biography of F. X. Garneau, and has published a thesis on *L'administration de la Nouvelle France.* The Rev. A. G. Morice has written in three volumes, *L'histoire de l'Église Catholique dans l'ouest canadien*. Séraphin Marion has told the life of a Canadian pioneer, *Pierre Boucher*. The Abbé Azarie Couillard-Després is the author of a number of genealogical and regional monographs: *Louis Hébert, Histoire de la famille et de la seigneurie de Saint Ours,* and *Histoire de Sorel*. Pierre Georges Roy, the archivist, has revealed, in a large number of publications, the riches in the historical documents in Canadian archives.

Fiction

Novels, which were rather rare in the nineteenth century, have become numerous in the last twenty years. The novel of Canadian manners, in which is depicted both life and nature in the various regions of the province of Quebec, has greatly benefited by the immense success obtained in Canada and in France by *Maria Chapdeleine,* which was written by a French author, Louis Hémon (1880-1913), who came to Canada to observe the life of the colonist.

Ernest Choquette, who before 1900 published *Les Ribaud* and *Claude Paysan,* wrote subsequently the novel entitled *La terre,* in which he aimed at attracting to rural life the young people of Quebec. Robert de Roquebrune made his *début* with the historical novel *Les habits rouges,* which deals with the rebellion of 1837-8; he followed this with *D'un océan d l'autre,* which tells the story of the life of the métis of the west; and in *Les dames Le Marchand* he approaches the psychological novel.

Harry Bernard has written society novels and novels of manners in *L'homme tombé, La terre vivante, La maison vide, Juana ma bien-aimée,* and *Dolorès*. The Abbé Lionel Groulx, under the penname of Alonié de Lestres, has written two novels with a patriotic theme,

L'appel de la race and *Au Cap Blomidon.* Georges Bugnet, under the pen-name of "Henri d'Outrement", tells the story of life in the west in a short story entitled *Le pin du Kaskeg* and in a novel entitled *Nipsya.* Claude Henri Grignon has written a character novel, *Un homme et son péché,* which is a good psychological study of the miser, and a collection of short stories entitled *Le déserteur.* Other novels worthy of mention are Leo Paul Desrosiers 's *Nord- sud,* the Rev. Adélard Dugré's *La campagne canadienne,* Damase Potvin's *Le membre, Le français,* and *La robe noire,* Robert Choquette's *La pension Leblanc,* Pierre Dupuy's *André Lawrence,* Antonio Proulx's *Le coeur est le maître,* and Ubald Paquin's *Jules Faubert* and *Le Paria.*

Philosophy, Sociology, and Oratory

In the spheres of philosophical and political thought, some writers and speakers have left important works. Mgr. Louis Adolphe Paquet occupies a foremost place with his studies of public law and social philosophy, *Principes généraux de droit public de l'Église, L'Église et l'éducation, L'organisation religieuse et le pouvoir civil,* and *L'action religieuse et la loi civile.* He has published, under the general title of *Études et appréciations,* works which deal with questions relative to apologetics and sociology: *Fragments apologétiques, Mélanges canadiens, Thèmes sociaux, Nouveaux fragments apologétiques* and *Nouveaux thèmes sociaux.* Both an orator and a theologian, Mgr. Paquet has brought together in one volume his *Discours et allocutions,* and he had published in two volumes *Un cours d'éloquence sacrée.* Edmond de Nevers (1862-1906) has left a work at once historical and sociological in *L'âme américaine.* He had previously published some thoughts on social order in his L'avenir du peuple canadien français, Errol

Bouchette was one of the forerunners of the school of economists, with his publications entitled *Emparons-nous de l'industrie, L'évolution économique de la province de Québec,* and *L'indépendance économique du Canada français.* At the same time, Léon Gérin was publishing his methodical observations on geography and social economy, *L'habitant de Saint-Justin* and *Deux familles rurales de la rive sud du Saint-Laurent.* Arthur Saint-Pierre is the author of a number of works on the labour question and professional organization.

Edouard Montpetit discusses the principles of political economy in *Pour tine doctrine* and some of their applications in *Sous le signe de l'or,* and *Les cordons de la bourse.*The Rev. Joseph Papin Archambault makes short and judicious contributions to the study of sociology and economics, both as the editor of *Les semaines sociales du Canada,* and as the author of monographs on *Les syndicats catholiques, Le devoir professionel,* and *Esquisses sociales.* Hermas Bastien deals with some philosophical problems in his *Essai sur la psychologie religieuse de William James* and his *Itinéraires philosophiques.*

It is to the treatment of social and political questions that French-Canadian eloquence has most often been devoted. In this connection two orators must be mentioned, Mgr. Paul Eugène Roy and Henri Bourassa. Mgr. Roy, who was archbishop of Quebec, founded at Quebec L'Action Sociale Catholique, and he expounded its programme and defended its doctrine in a series of vigorous and solidly built addresses published after his death. He was the author of *Discours religieux et patriotiques, l'Action Sociale Catholique et tempérance,* and *Apôtres et apostolat.* We owe to him also some works of religious eloquence, and a correspondence entitled *D'une âme à un autre.* Henri Bourassa has been at once a journalist and a tribune of the people. He founded *Le Devoir,* and he has expounded on the hustings and in the legislature, both at Quebec and at Ottawa, his political doctrines. The rights of the French race in Canada, economic problems, religious and social questions have in turn called forth his articles and his speeches. Both articles and speeches have had an immediate success. They are written in an animated and sometimes violent style, which captures attention. They have been collected in a large number of pamphlets, among which may be mentioned the following: *Que devons-nous d l'Angleterre; Hier, aujourd'hui, demain; Le pape arbitre de la paix,* and *La langue gardienne de la foi.*

Chroniques, Narratives, and Criticism

The literature of the *chronique* and of literary criticism is voluminous. Narratives of the soil have been particularly successful. They have often been called forth, like the poetry of the soil, by the studies of the Société du Parler Français au Canada. Among these writers of *chroniques* and *récits* should be mentioned Adjutor Rivard, the founder of the Société du Parler Français, who has painted the picturesque scenes of Canadian life in his *Chez nous* and *Chez nos gens,* and who is also the author of *Études sur les parlers de France au Canada.* The Rev. Louis Lalande has sketched, with some originality his *Silhouettes paroissiales,* and he is also the author of a volume of religious and patriotic addresses entitled *Au service de la famille.* Brother Marie-Victorin, who is a botanist, describes the flowers and the landscapes and the life of French Canada in his *Récits laurentiens* and his *Croquis laurentiens.* Louis Philippe Geoffrion, secretary of the Société du Parler

Français au Canada, has gathered his observations on the popular speech of the French-Canadian people in his volumes of *Zigzags autour de nos parlers.* Mgr. Camille Roy, in his *Propos canadiens* and *Etudes et croquis,* has described the landscape or outlined the scenes of life in French Canada.

The Abbé Lionel Groulx has grouped memories of life, history, and manners in his *Rapaillages* and his *Chez nos ancêtres.* Georges Bouchard has told of *Vieilles choses et vieilles gens.* Brother Gilles has written for Canadian readers about *Les choses qui s'en vont.* Claude Melançon leads the reader *Parterre et par eau.* Father Hugolin brings together in *Horizons et pensées* and in *Dans le cloître et par le monde* short tales and impressions. Some women who write *chroniques* in the newspapers have collected them in books. Mention may be made of Mme.

Raoul Dandurand's *Le coin de feu,* of *Les chroniques du Lundi* and *Fleurs champêtres,* by Robertine Barry ("Françoise") of *Première péché* and *Le long du chemin,* by Mme. Huguenin {"Madeleine"}, of *Lettres de Fadette,* by Mme. Saint-Jacques, of *Autour de la maison* and *Couleur du temps,* by Michelle Le Normand, and of *L'art d'être heureuse,* by Mme. D. Frémont ("Annette Saint-Amand").

One must give a high place, among writers of *chroniques* and of essays to the Abbé Henri Beaudé (1870-1930). The Abbé Beaudé. who wrote under the pseudonym of "Henri d'Arles", was a writer of delicate and subtle style, careful of detail and of colour, with a fine and chiselled art of expression. He has left, among other works, *Propos d'art, Pastels, Arabesques, Laudes, Miscellanées,* and *Horizons.* He also indulged in literary criticism; and we find this in *Essais et conférences; Eaux fortes et tailles douces; Nos historiens; Louis Fréchette,* and *Etampes.*

Literary criticism began with the dawn of the twentieth century. Mgr. Camille Roy was one of the pioneers in this field, and he has helped by his historical researches and by his criticisms of Canadian literature to make the literature of French Canada, both past and present, better known. He is the author of *Essais sur la littérature canadienne; Nouveaux essais; Nos origines littéraires; Erables en fleurs; A l'ombre des érables; Regards sur les lettres;* and *Histoire de la littérature canadienne.* To him we owe also a collection of speeches, *Les leçons de notre histoire.*

Louis Dantin is one of the chief of the group of literary critics, and one of those who analyse with the greatest insight and weight the books that appear. He has published two volumes on *Les poètes de l'Amérique française* and *Gloses critiques.* He is also a poet, and writes short stories. These are gathered in *La vie en rêve.* Among the numerous critics who study present-day French-Canadian literature, mention should be made of Jean Charles Harvey, the author of *Pages de critique,* of the Rev. Émile Chartier, who wrote *Pages de combat,* of Maurice Hébert, the writer of *De livres en livres* and *D'un livre à un autre,* of Harry Bernard, with his *Essais critiques,* of Marcel Dugas, who has published *La littérature canadienne* and an authoritative study of *Louis Fréchette,* of Séraphin Marion, who has brought together his principal studies in *En feuilletant nos écrivains,* and of Alfred Des Rochers, with his *Paragraphes.*

This survey of the principal writers in French-Canadian literature and of their chief works shows that French-Canadian literature is in process of full growth.

It goes hand in hand with the history of the French-Canadian people, whether to tell that history or to illustrate it. Written in the French language, it is yet allied to the literature of the English tongue in Canada; and it bears witness, with the English-Canadian literature, to the intellectual life of Canada. Both literatures are necessary to the complete life of the Canadian people.

4

Canadian Poetry

There are three distinct branches of Canadian poetry: French-Canadian poetry (mostly written by *Québécois* authors), First Nations poetry and English-Canadian poetry.

English-Canadian Poetry

Beginnings

The earliest works of poetry, mainly written by visitors, described the new territories in optimistic terms, mainly targeted at a European audience. One of the first works was Robert Hayman's *Quodlibets,* composed in Newfoundland and published in 1628.

With the growth of English language communities near the end of the 18th century, poetry aimed at local readers began to appear in local newspapers. These writings were mainly intended to reflect the prevailing cultural values of the time and were modeled after English poetry of the same period.

In the first half of the 19th century, poetic works began to reflect local subjects. *Acadia* by Joseph Howe and *The Saint Lawrence and the Saguenay* by Charles Sangster are examples of this trend. Early nationalistic verses were composed by writers including Thomas D'Arcy McGee. Many "regional" poets also espoused the British political and aesthetic jingoism of the period. For example, High Tory loyalist & occasional poet Thomas H. Higginson of Vankleek Hill, Ontario, produced paeons to Sir Francis Bond Head (Wm. Lyon Mackenzie's opponent) and the British war effort in the Crimea (such as *Sonnet to Florence Nightingale* and others), while producing some interesting nature verse exemplifying the all-pervasive influence of Wordsworth's view of nature and the sublime.

Confederation

A group of poets now known as the "Confederation Poets" began writing following the formation of the new Dominion of Canada in 1867, including Charles G. D. Roberts, Archibald Lampman, Bliss Carman and Duncan Campbell Scott. Choosing the world of nature as their inspiration, their work was drawn from their own experiences and, at its best, written in their own tones.

Early 20th Century

During this period, E. Pauline Johnson and Robert W. Service were writing popular poetry - Johnson's based on her English and Mohawk heritage and Service writing tales of the Yukon gold rush. In 1915, John McCrae, serving as a surgeon in the Canadian Army, wrote the famous war poem "In Flanders Fields".

In Newfoundland, E.J. Pratt described the struggle to make a living on the land in poems about maritime life and the history of Canada. Meanwhile, in central Canada, poets such as Ralph Gustafson and Raymond Knister were moving away from traditional verse forms. Pauline Johnson was born on March 10, 1861 near Brantford, Ontario. She became a much-loved poet in the late 19th & early 20th centuries, writing both her Aboriginal and European roots.

In the 1930s, A.J.M. Smith and F.R. Scott helped inspire the development of new poetic voices in Montreal through the *McGill Fortnightly Review* and the anthology *New Provinces*. The "new poetry" valued intellect over sentimentality, or as some have put it, logic over human emotions.

Under the editorship (literary) of Earle Birney, the *Canadian Forum* helped promote similar developments in Toronto. Dorothy Livesay, born in Manitoba, was an important contributor to the Toronto movement. These two urban centres of literary activity provided fertile ground for the development of later poets such as Irving Layton and Raymond Souster.

Post War

Following World War II, a new breed of poets appeared, writing for a well-educated audience. These included James Reaney, Jay Macpherson and Leonard Cohen. Meanwhile, some maturing authors such as Layton, Souster, Harold Standish and Louis Dudek, moved in a different direction, adopting colloquial speech in their work.

In the 1960s, a renewed sense of nation helped foster new voices: Margaret Atwood, Michael Ondaatje, Leonard Cohen, Eli Mandel and Margaret Avison. Others such as Al Purdy, Milton Acorn, and Earle Birney, already published, produced some of their best work during this period.

The TISH Poetry movement in Vancouver brought about poetic innovation from bpNichol, Jamie Reid,

George Bowering, Fred Wah, Frank Davey, Daphne Marlatt, David Cull, and Lionel Kearns.

Since the 1990s, several Governor General's Award-winning poets, in particular Jan Zwicky and Tim Lilburn, have been engaged in nonfiction writing that maps the relationships between poetry and philosophy. Zwicky's "Lyric Philosophy" and "Wisdom and Metaphor", as well as Lilburn's collection "Thinking and Singing", are representative works.

A younger generation of Canadian poets has been expanding the boundaries of originality: Ken Babstock, Karen Solie, Sonnet L'Abbé, George Elliott Clarke and Barry Dempster have all imprinted their unique consciousnesses onto the map of Canadian imagery. Evie Christie's collection, *Gutted,* seems to evoke the 17th century metaphysical conceit, but in a modern, urban Canadian guise.

Uniquely Canadian Forms

The Viator poem form was invented by Canadian author and poet, Robin Skelton. It consists of any stanzaic form in which the first line of the first stanza is the second line of the second stanza and so on until the poem ends with the line with which it began. The term, *Viator* comes from the Latin for *traveller.* An example of Skelton's form may be found in his excellent reference book, *The Shapes of our Singing,* and is entitled *Dover Beach Revisited.*

French-Canadian Poetry

Early Verse

The first book written in verse by a Canadian was

Épîtres, Satires, Chansons, Épigrammes et Autres Pièces de vers by Michel Bibaud, published in 1830.

Mouvement Littéraire

A group of French speaking poets and authors belonging to the Mouvement littéraire came to Ottawa from Quebec City when the civil service moved to Ottawa in 1870. This group included Alfred Garneau, Antoine Gerin-Lajoie, Achilles Frechette and others. They are considered some of the most important poets and writers in 19th Century French Canada.

End of 19th Century

Octave Crémazie is considered the father of French Canadian poetry. His poetry and that of his follower Louis Fréchette are romantic of form and patriotic in inspiration. At the same time, Pamphile Le May was writing intimist poetry about the simple farm life and Alfred Garneau wrote his feelings.

The Montreal School

L'École littéraire de Montréal is not a literary school *per se* but more of a group of poets that met regularly. In reaction to the earlier following of the romantic Victor Hugo, they took later schools as their masters. The most talented among them was certainly Émile Nelligan, a young poet who stopped writing at only 20 years of age due to mental illness.

The Terroir

Outside Montreal, other poets, such as Nérée Beauchemin continued Pamphile Le May's depiction of the life of the *habitants*. Then came the powerful Alfred Desrochers, a precursor to the "pays" school of poetry of Gaston Miron John PauL Ambas.

5

Canadian Fictions

Science Fiction

A strong element in contemporary Canadian culture is rich, diverse, thoughtful and witty science fiction. Possibly the first recorded Canadian work of science fiction is the 1896 *Tisab Ting, or, The Electrical Kiss,* a pseudonynous first novel by a Ida May Ferguson of New Brunswick under the pseudonym "Dyjan Fergus." Set in late 20th century Montreal, it features an "electrical genius": a "learned Chinaman" who woos and wins a Canadian wife through his superior scientific knowledge as embodied in "the Electrical Kiss". It is of interest mainly because of its early publication date; a microfiche reprint was issued in 1980.

Like many aspects of Canadian culture, Canadian science fiction emerged from a variety of isolated sources, including A. E. van Vogt, the fantasy works of John Buchan, the poetry of Phyllis Gotlieb, and a handful of other writers. In the late 20th century, political upheaval in the United States brought such talents as Spider Robinson and Judith Merril to Canada.

In 1973, the World Science Fiction Convention was held again in Toronto, bringing a new generation of interest to writers like Judith and Garfield Reeves-Stevens. This led to a range of activities and interest in the genre. Merril began hosting quarterly gatherings of authors in a loose group called "Toronto Hydra", a tradition she had brought from the New York SF community.

In the early 1980s, the Ontario Science Fiction Club was set up by Robert J. Sawyer, while the Bunch of Seven became the first known science fiction writing circle in Canada, helping the success of authors like S.M. Stirling and Tanya Huff, which later led to the Cecil Street Irregulars that included writers like Cory Doctorow. Charles de Lint and then Guy Gavriel Kay became notable for using Canadian settings in science fiction and fantasy, and William Gibson pioneered the cyberpunk subgenre with his novel *Neuromancer*.

In Quebec, Élisabeth Vonarburg and other authors developed a related tradition of French-Canadian SF. The Prix Boreal was established in 1979 to honour Canadian science fiction works in French. The Aurora Awards (briefly preceded by the Casper Award) were founded in 1980 to recognize and promote the best works of Canadian science fiction in both French and English.

Regular annual science fiction conventions, notably Ad Astra, brought fans and writers together to further broaden awareness and appreciation of science fiction literature in Canada.

By the 1990s, Canadian science fiction was well established and internationally recognized; mainstream authors such as Margaret Atwood began including SF in their repertoire.

The Canadian Broadcasting Company began producing science fiction as early as the 1950s. CTV produced The Starlost at the CFTO studios in Scarborough. In the early 1990s, Toronto and Vancouver became prominent centres of television and film production, with shows like Forever Knight and Robocop, then The X-Files raised the profile of Canadian science fiction television much higher. By the late 1990s, a significant fraction of science fiction and fantasy on television was produced in Canada. In the early 2000s, due to changes in tax laws, production companies shifted much of their operations from Toronto to Vancouver.

Feminist Science Fiction

Feminist science fiction is a sub-genre of science fiction which tends to deal with women's roles in society. Feminist science fiction poses questions about social issues such as how society constructs gender roles, the role reproduction plays in defining gender and the unequal political and personal power of men and women. Some of the most notable feminist science fiction works have illustrated these themes using utopias to explore a society in which gender differences or gender power imbalances do not exist, or dystopias to explore worlds in which gender inequalities are intensified, thus asserting a need for feminist work to continue. According to Elyce Rae Helford:

> "Science fiction and fantasy serve as important vehicles for feminist thought, particularly as bridges between theory and practice. No other genres so actively invite representations of the ultimate goals of feminism: worlds free of sexism, worlds in which women's contributions (to science) are recognized

and valued, worlds in which the diversity of women's desire and sexuality, and worlds that move beyond gender

Women writers have played key roles in science fiction and fantasy literature, often addressing themes of gender. One of the first writers of science fiction was Mary Shelley, whose novel *Frankenstein* dealt with the asexual creation of new life, a re-telling of the Adam and Eve story.

Women writers in the utopian literature movement of the nineteenth and early twentieth centuries, at the time of first wave feminism, often addressed sexism. Charlotte Perkins Gilman did so in *Herland* (1915), for example. *The Sultana's Dream* (1905) by Bengali Muslim feminist, Roquia Sakhawat Hussain, depicts a gender-reversed purdah in an alternate and terminologically futuristic world. During the 1920s writers such as Clare Winger Harris and Gertrude Barrows Bennett published science fiction stories written from female perspectives and occasionally dealt with gender and sexuality based topics. Meanwhile, much pulp science fiction published during 1920s and 1930s carried an exaggerated view of masculinity along with sexist portrayals of women. By the 1960s science fiction was combining sensationalism with political and technological critiques of society. With the advent of feminism, women's roles were questioned in this "subversive, mind expanding genre."

Two notable texts early in second wave feminism are Ursula K. Le Guin's *The Left Hand of Darkness* (1969) and Joanna Russ' *The Female Man* (1970). Each highlights the socially constructed aspects of gender roles by creating worlds with genderless societies. Both authors were pioneers in feminist criticism of science fiction during the 1960s and 70s through essays collected in *The Language of the Night* (Le Guin, 1979) and *How To Suppress Women's Writing* (Russ, 1983).

Margaret Atwood's *Handmaid's Tale* tells a dystopic tale of a society in which women have been systematically stripped of all liberty, and was motivated by fear of potential retrogressive effects on women's rights stemming from the feminist backlash of the 1980s. Octavia Butler poses complicated questions about the nature of race and gender in *Kindred* (1979).

By the 1970s the science fiction community was confronting questions of feminism and sexism within science fiction culture itself. Multiple Hugo-winning fan writer and professor of literature Susan Wood and others organized the "feminist panel" at the 1976 World Science Fiction Convention against considerable resistance. Reactions to the appearance of feminists among fannish ranks led indirectly to the creation of *A Women's APA* and WisCon.

Feminist science fiction is sometimes taught at the university level to explore the role of social constructs in understanding gender.

Feminist science fiction is evidenced in the globally popular mediums of comic books, manga, and graphic novels. In the early 1960s, Marvel Comics already contained some strong female characters, although they often suffered from stereotypical female weakness such as fainting after intense exertion. By the 1970s and 1980s, true female heroes started to emerge on the pages of comics. This was helped by the emergence of self-identified feminist writers including Ann Nocenti, Linda Fite, and Barbara Kesel. As female visibility in comics increased, the "fainting heroine" type began to fade into the past. However, some female comic book writers, such as Gail Simone, believe that female characters are still relegated to plot devices.

One of the first appearances of a strong female character was that of Wonder Woman co-created by husband and wife team William Moulton Marston and Elizabeth Holloway Marston. In December 1941, Wonder Woman came to life on the pages of *All Star Comics* volume eight. The character later spawned a television series starring Lynda Carter and a *film adaptation* is currently underway. Feminism in science fiction shôjo manga has been a theme in the works of Moto Hagio among others, for whom the writings of Ursula K. Le Guin have been a major influence.

Historical Fiction

According to Huck et al. historical fiction encompasses "all realistic stories that are set in the past". Egoff and Saltman also endorse this definition and thereby exclude "past-time fantasies." There is some controversy around this point. Children's author Heather Kirk contends that it is unreasonable to exclude, as Egoff and Saltman do, novels which involve time travel, in which a contemporary protagonist travels to the past and takes part in events there. Following this definition, Egoff and Saltman exclude important historical novels such as Karleen Bradford's *The Other Elizabeth,* Janet Lunn's *Root Cellar,* and Kevin Major's *Blood Red Ochre* from the historical fiction category and include them instead in their "Fantasy" chapter. As Kirk points out, this problem would be merely academic if it did not result in important historical novels being overlooked.

Children's fiction writer Jill Paton Walsh distinguishes between the historical novel, which is one that is "wholly or partly about public events and social conditions which are the material of history" and the 'costume' novel, which simply chooses a place and time from the past as stage props. She asks, "Can we imagine the plot and characters set in any other period? If we can, then the book is not in any organic way *about* its historical period. It may be a very good book, but it is not a historical novel". Kit Pearson's *Guests of War* trilogy, the story of two British children sent to Toronto during World War Two, is an outstanding example of the former. Kirk calls it, "complex and mature in subject matter, discussing as it does the results of peaceful colonialism on the mentality of Canadians during World War II: the unquestioned loyalty to Britain, the indifference to the plight of Jewish and Dutch children, the smugness about our own safety and affluence, and the incomprehension of the emotional trauma caused by first-hand experience of war". It is firmly set in its time and place. Egoff and Saltman would consider the first two books of Marianne Brandis' trilogy, *The Tinderbox* and *The Quarter-Pie Window* as "costume novels." (The third book was not yet published.) They describe these books as "not contain[ing] the slightest mention of a historical event (a war or rebellion) or a social situation (the plight of homeless boys or labour disputes). These are individual life stories that could take place today but are set in the past".

New Developments

There has been increased emphasis on historical fiction among writers of children's and adolescent fiction over the past twenty-five years. This interest is increasing rather than waning.. In the past year, fictional diaries, novellas, full-fledged novels, and re-issued stories by authors such as G.A. Henty and Ralph Connor, have all appeared.

Along with this renewed interest, there have been several new developments. One is the proliferation of female protagonists. Jane Austen had a character say, "[History] tells me nothing that does not either vex me or weary me.... the men are all so good for nothing and hardly any women at al". The problem of lack of women, or at least girls, has been largely rectified in Canadian juvenile fiction over the past decade. (The "good for nothing" men may still be there!) In fact, it might be fair to say that females have taken over. Two new series support this point. Four new novellas in the *Our Canadian Girl* series have been published to date, each featuring a ten-year-old girl. The two books in the *Dear Canada,* which are presently in print, have female protagonists. There are countless other examples.

Another trend is the blurring of the line between fiction and nonfiction. Barbara Greenwood, for example, has published several books, including *Gold Rush Fever* (2001), which include historical background information woven around a fictional narrative. *The Story of Canada* (1992), a reference book for a juvenile audience, contains stories. Interestingly enough, this book was written by a children's fiction author, Janet Lunn, and a historian, Christopher Moore.

This trend is also evident in recently published journals. These publications range from pure fiction, to fictionalized presentation of the life of an actual person, to an authentic journal embellished with insertions by a contemporary author/editor. For instance, the books of the *Dear Canada* series, with titles like *Orphan at My Door: The Home Child Diary of Victoria Cope* (2001), sound like actual journals. They are written in the first person and presented as children's diaries, but are in fact, pure fiction.

Eleonora's Diary (1994), is the authentic journal of a young girl, written over thirteen years, and preserved by her family for 150 years. Caroline Parry provides lengthy explanations of the historical background to events described by Eleonora, a glossary of archaic terms, photographs, maps, and an ongoing discussion of how she is going about constructing an historical record of Eleonora's life.

Biography, too, has come into its own recently. Here, too, there is great variation in approach. Susan Merritt's *Her Story: Women from Canada's Past* (1993, 1995, 1999), now in three volumes, fits within the traditional biography genre. Connie Brummel Crook's three-volume biography of Nellie McClung (1994, 1998, 1999), however, is fictionalized. The author builds a story around documented events, constructing dialogue and inventing other events in order to move the story along and keep it interesting.

Concerns

So far we have discussed a few points around historical fiction which are of interest to any student of the subject. But what are the concerns of special relevance to teachers of history? Two are particularly important: accuracy and presentism. Accuracy is a concern when using historical fiction because its prime purposes are to tell a story and to entertain, not to provide information. Charles Frasier (2001), author of the adult novel, *Cold Mountain*, talks about this:

> Not long ago I met a reader who told me her husband was convinced that at some point in *Cold Mountain*, I began making things up. Her husband wondered when that was. I said I knew exactly at what point I began making things up. It was on page one. That exchange keeps coming back to me, largely

> because its assumptions raise any number of questions... about how historical fiction works and, indeed, what its goals as a genre should be. Where, for example, should we place the balance point between the history and the fiction? (I'm supposing, perhaps unfairly, that the husband would position it to leave a great weighty length of history and only a bare nub of fiction, just enough to keep the plot rolling along.) Might we wish to limit historical fiction to a retelling — or repackaging —of so-called actual past events? To what extent are we writers free to introduce well-known historical figures into our work and have them carry on conversations and commit acts we cannot verify? Are we free to lash them with emotions they never actually felt it worked best for me to let the fiction drive and the history ride.

A novel should never be the sole information source about a particular place, time, or event. Also, we should encourage students to view information provided in novels from a critical perspective. However, it should be noted that, at the same time, students should not be viewing textbooks and other nonfiction reference books, uncritically either. As with novels, they should be examining nonfiction resources for what is omitted as well as for what is included; and for how information is presented, so they can determine whose views are given a prominent place.

It is important that we make students aware of the author's prime purposes; that is, storytelling and entertainment rather than provision of information; and that we encourage students to read historical novels primarily for the enjoyment they offer. As Roberta McKay has pointed out, literature should be used to "provoke an aesthetic response, to stir an affinity with the human condition, to capture our hearts and imaginations as well as our minds, and to connect us to ourselves and others." It should be noted too, that, in spite of their desire to "let the fiction drive," many authors report taking great delight in amassing the historical details necessary to paint a rich and (mostly) accurate picture of the past. Well known author Jean Little has said:

> It is the small details that make historical fiction work, I believe. You need to know what hymns they sang, what their family traditions were, what sayings were passed down, what riddles were set, what advice was given to children, what chores they had to do, what books they read, what games they played, what gave them nightmares. Finding these bits and pieces is like going on a treasure hunt-deeply satisfying when you stumble on a tiny bit that brings your whole scene to life.

Janet McNaughton, author of *To Dance at the Palais Royale* (1997) has commented on some of the questions around accuracy which she confronted when writing this novel. In the end she placed the "message" she wished to send to her young readers over the accuracy of the information she provided.

For instance, she manipulated circumstances in order to portray interactions between the British born protagonist, Aggie and Rachel Mendorfsky, a Jewish woman from Russia.. It is unlikely that such interactions would ever have actually taken place. She explained that "Toronto was on the verge of becoming one of the great cosmopolitan cities of all time. And in an odd way, I felt it would be untrue to the future if my view of the past portrayed Toronto as nothing but that outpost of the empire". And yet, Toronto in the 1920s was indeed an "outpost of Empire." McNaughton manipulated her story in order to portray the city that Toronto would become rather than the city as it was during the period in which the events of the novel took place. It seems an odd decision.

The other concern is "presentism." This refers to the placing of "present-day culturally contingent values and conventions and judgments upon the people of the past, people whose cultural frameworks were quite different".

Authors often use "presentism" quite intentionally because it is a means of making protagonists more convincing and realistic to their contemporary readers. They become recognizable as people the reader might know, but who just happen to be operating in an historical context. Many authors of juvenile fiction get around this difficulty by using the device discussed earlier; this is having children go back in time, and thus legitimately view events from a contemporary perspective.

McNaughton has described how she struggled, in *To Dance at the Palais Royale,* with the question of how to present an action which would be considered child abuse today; but which was perfectly acceptable, and even laudable, parental behaviour in 1920s Scotland. The younger children in the family steal from the collection plate at church, and are whipped by their father as punishment.

She had to include this action because it was appropriate to the time. However, she wanted her readers to realize that she did not approve. In the end, she compromised. She had the Minister approve of the father's actions, thereby showing that they were acceptable within that community in that historical period. However, she had Aggie, the novel's protagonist, strongly disapprove.

6

Literary Works of Robertson Davies

William Robertson Davies (born August 28, 1913, at Thamesville, Ontario, and died December 2, 1995 at Orangeville, Ontario) was a Canadian novelist, playwright, critic, journalist, and professor. He was one of Canada's best-known and most popular authors, and one of its most distinguished "men of letters", a term Davies is variously said to have gladly accepted for himself and to have detested. Davies was the founding Master of Massey College, a graduate residential college associated with the University of Toronto.

Early Life

Growing up, Davies was surrounded by books and language. His father, Senator William Rupert Davies, was a newspaperman, and both parents were voracious readers. He, in turn, read everything he could. He also participated in theatrical productions as a child, where he developed a lifelong interest in drama.

He attended Upper Canada College in Toronto from 1926 to 1932 and while there attended services at the Church of St. Mary Magdalene. He would later leave the Presbyterian Church and convert to Anglicanism over objections to Calvinist theology. Davies later used his experience of the ceremonial of High Mass at St Mary Magdalene's in his novel *The Cunning Man*.

After Upper Canada College, he studied at Queen's University in Kingston, Ontario from 1932 until 1935. At Queen's he was enrolled as a special student not working towards a degree, and wrote for the student paper, *The Queen's Journal*. He left Canada to study at Balliol College, Oxford, where he received a BLitt degree in 1938. The next year he published his thesis, *Shakespeare's Boy Actors*, and embarked on an acting career outside London. In 1940 he played small roles and did literary work for the director at the Old Vic Repertory Company in London. Also that year Davies married Australian Brenda Mathews, whom he had met at Oxford, and who was then working as stage manager for the theatre.

Davies' early life provided him with themes and material to which he would often return in his later work, including the theme of Canadians returning to England to finish their education, and the theatre.

Middle Years

Davies and his new bride returned to Canada in 1940, where he took the position of literary editor at the magazine Saturday Night. Two years later, he became editor of the *Peterborough Examiner* in the small city of Peterborough, Ontario, northeast of Toronto. Again he was able to mine his experiences here for many of the characters and situations which later appeared in his novels and plays.

Davies, along with family members William Rupert Davies and Arthur Davies, purchased several media outlets. Along with the *Examiner* newspaper, they owned the *Kingston Whig-Standard* newspaper, CHEX-AM, CKWS-AM, CHEX-TV, and CKWS-TV.

During his tenure as editor of the *Examiner*, which lasted from 1942 to 1955, and when he was publisher from 1955 to 1965, Davies published a total of 18 books, produced several of his own plays and wrote articles for various journals.

For example, Davies set out his theory of acting in his *Shakespeare for Young Players* (1947) and then put theory into practice when he wrote *Eros at Breakfast*, a one-act play which was named best Canadian play of the year by the 1948 Dominion Drama Festival.

Eros at Breakfast was followed in close succession by *Fortune, My Foe* in 1949 and *At My Heart's Core*, a three-act play, in 1950. Meanwhile, Davies was writing humorous essays in the *Examiner* under the pseudonym Samuel Marchbanks. Some of these were collected and published in *The Diary of Samuel Marchbanks* (1947), *The Table Talk of Samuel Marchbanks* (1949), and later in *Samuel Marchbanks' Almanack* (1967). (An omnibus edition of the three Marchbanks books, with new notes by the author, was published under the title *The Papers of Samuel Marchbanks* in 1985.)

Also during the 1950s, Davies played a major role in launching the Stratford Shakespearean Festival of Canada. He served on the Festival's board of governors and collaborated with the Festival's director, Sir Tyrone Guthrie, in publishing three books about the Festival's early years.

Although his first love was drama and he had achieved some success with his occasional humorous essays, Davies found greater success in fiction. His first three novels, which later became known as The Salterton Trilogy, were *Tempest-Tost* (1951), *Leaven of Malice* (1954) (which won the Stephen Leacock Award for Humour), and *A Mixture of Frailties* (1958). These novels explored the difficulty of sustaining a cultural life in Canada, and life on a small-town newspaper, subjects of which Davies had first-hand knowledge.

The 1960s

In 1960 Davies joined Trinity College at the University of Toronto, where he would teach literature until 1981. The following year he published a collection of essays on literature *A Voice From the Attic*, and was awarded the Lorne Pierce Medal for his literary achievements.

In 1963 he became the Master of Massey College, the University of Toronto's new graduate college. During his stint as Master, he initiated the tradition of writing and telling ghost stories at the yearly Christmas celebrations. His stories were later collected in his book *High Spirits* (1982).

The 1970s

Davies drew on his interest in Jungian psychology to create what is perhaps his greatest novel: *Fifth Business* (1970), a book that draws heavily on Davies' own experiences, his love of myth and magic and his knowledge of small-town mores. The narrator, like Davies, is of immigrant Canadian background, with a father who runs the town paper. The book's characters act in roles that roughly correspond to Jungian archetypes according to Davies' belief in the predominance of the spirit over the things of the world.

Davies built on the success of *Fifth Business* with two more novels: *The Manticore* (1972), a novel cast largely in the form of a Jungian analysis (for which he received that year's Governor-General's Literary Award), and *World of Wonders* (1975). Together these three books came to be known as The Deptford Trilogy.

The 1980s and 1990s

When Davies retired from his position at the University, his seventh novel, a satire of academic life, *The Rebel Angels* (1981), was published, followed by *What's Bred in the Bone* (1985). These two books, along with *The Lyre of Orpheus,* became known as The Cornish Trilogy.

During his retirement he continued to write novels which further established him as a major figure in the literary world: *The Lyre of Orpheus* (1988), *Murther and Walking Spirits* (1991) and *The Cunning Man* (1994). A third novel in what would have been a further trilogy was in progress at Davies' death. He also realized a long-held dream when he penned the libretto to an opera: *The Golden Ass,* based on *The Metamorphoses* of Lucius Apuleius, just like that written by one of the characters in Davies' 1958 *A Mixture of Frailties.* The opera was performed by the Canadian Opera Company at the Hummingbird Centre in Toronto, in April, 1999, several years after Davies' death.

Davies was a fine public speaker: deft, often humorous, and unafraid to be unfashionable. Often asked if he used a computer, Davies said in 1987: "I don't want a word-processor. I process my own words. Helpful people assure me that a word-processor would save me a great deal of time. But I don't want to save time. I want to write the best book I can, and I have whatever time it takes to make that attempt". In its obituary The Times wrote: 'Davies encompassed all the great elements of life...His novels combined deep seriousness and psychological inquiry with fantasy and exuberant mirth.'

Fifth Business

Fifth Business is the masterpiece of Robertson Davies. It is the first installment of the Deptford Trilogy and is a story of the life of the narrator, Dunstan Ramsay. It is Davies' best-known novel, and considered his finest. First published by Macmillan of Canada in 1970, *Fifth Business* was selected 40th on the American Modern Library's "reader's list" of the 100 best novels of the 20th century.

Plot

Ramsay's passion for hagiology and his guilty connection to Mary Dempster provide most of the impetus and background for this novel. He spends much of the book struggling with his image of Mary Dempster as a fool-saint and dealing with issues of guilt that spawned from a childhood accident. The entire story is told in the form of a letter written by Ramsay on his retirement from teaching at Colborne College, addressed to the school Headmaster.

Epigraph

Those roles which, being neither those of hero nor Heroine, Confidante nor Villain, but which were none the less essential to bring about the Recognition or the denouement were called the Fifth Business in drama and Opera companies organized according to the old style; the player who acted these parts was often referred to as Fifth Business. - Tho. Overskou, Den Danske Skueplads

Davies was pressured by his publisher to provide some clear idea of what exactly 'Fifth Business' was, and so Davies affixed this opening quotation, which was taken at face value for many years.

Part One - Mrs Dempster

The story of Dunstan Ramsay's life begins on 5:58 o'clock p.m. on 27 December 1908, when Dunstan was just a boy of ten years old, and at the time was called Dunstable. He and his lifelong friend and enemy Percy Boyd Staunton had been sledding together and had quarrelled, and on the way back to town Percy hid a rock in a snowball and threw it at Dunstable, but it hit the passing-by Mary Dempster. Mrs. Dempster is the wife of Deptford's Baptist minister, and she is also very pregnant. The shock of the stone hitting her head causes her to become slightly deranged, and she goes into labour to deliver a premature baby boy, Paul Dempster. Mr. Amasa Dempster is shown to be of no aid to his wife during the delivery as he Christens the child and prays to God to take his wife and spare his child, so it is up to Mrs. Ramsay to help Mrs. Dempster through this ordeal.

Dunstan steps back from his narrative to inform us as to the reason we are being treated to his life history. The year is now 1969, and Dunstan is writing to the headmaster of the Colbourne boy's school he had taught at to protest the tributary send-off he was given upon his retirement. The article summarizes some of the important details of Dunstan's life, including that (Percy) Boy Staunton has recently died and that Ramsay had a heart attack shortly after this event. Dunstan is referred to by the nickname 'corky', in reference to the wooden leg he carries after his debilitating service in WW1. It is also established that Dunstan has been teaching History, in an eccentric fashion, at this institution for 45 years. Dunstan takes insult to his portrayal in this article and the dismissal of his subject of 'mythic history', along with the lack of mention of his V.C. and six books. He wants to prove to the headmaster that he has in fact lead a rich and full life, in his own way, which Dunstan describes as being 'cast by Fate and my own character for the vital though never glorious role of Fifth Business!".

Dunstan returns to his description of his childhood to try and give us a sense of his hometown, Deptford, which is located in Southern Ontario, Canada, on the Thames river (in reality: Thamesville). 1900s Deptford contains 500-800 people divided between 5 churches. Dunstan's father is the owner and editor of the local paper, while Percy's father is a seldom-practicing doctor who is becoming rich by growing sugar-beets. They value cleanliness and each sects views themselves superior to the others, and they all view themselves as superior people compared to the even smaller and more rustic town down the road.

4. Returning to the infant Paul Dempster and Mrs. Ramsay's efforts to assist in his survival after having been born 80 days premature, Mrs. Ramsay builds a nest for the baby and scolds the reverend about his counterproductive prayers to God to take his hysterical wife from him. During this time Dunstable is at home suffering terrible fits of agony in the belief that he is responsible for Paul's birth and Mary's dementia

because he avoided a pain that was clearly intended for him and let someone else suffer in his place. Percy has denied all knowledge of what happened, and threatens Dunstable that he'd better forget to, for his own good. Dunstable denies knowing who threw the snowball when his parents confront him, and for the rest of his life he is haunted by this decision and wishes for death to end his suffering.

This section returns to descriptions of Deptford culture as the foolish Mary Dempster attempts to re-enter society after her traumatic experience. There is a general consensus about the town that the girl is not fit for the duty of being a minister's wife. Dunstable's mother ordered him over to the Dempster household to help with the chores that Mary is absentmindedly neglecting.

As he grows older, Dunstable's association with the ostracized Mary Dempster comes to hurt his popularity at school, and he discovers that his well-to-do rival Percy is one of the people snickering at him behind his back. But Dunstable has a trick for being able to get off 'good one' comebacks in fights, and knows that he can disarm Percy at any moment by telling the boys Mrs. Staunton's pet name for Percy: "Pidgy Boy-Boy". Dunstable has a crush on a girl named Leola Cruikshank, but he reflectively realizes that he was also in love with Mrs. Dempster and genuinely enjoyed helping at her house. Dunstable fights another boy in his class who refers to Mrs. Dempster's house as 'the bughouse'.

At age thirteen Dunstable gets a job at the local library, which suits his introverted interests very well. Dunstable absorbs the encyclopaedia and also explores the world of stage magic as explained by Houdini and

Hoffman. But the town does not place much value on knowledge, and even less for devilish conjuring, and this takes Dunstable into a quarrel with his mother. Dunstable comes to understand that there is darkness within the human soul, and that no one, not even his own mother, can be trusted.

Dunstable delves further into the realm of magic, and the miracles of the Catholic saints. And he shares these interests with the four year old Paul Dempster, who turns out to be much more proficient with simple slight-of-hand tricks then Dunstable could ever hope to be.

Dunstable next describes his feud with the Reverend Amasa Dempster, who believes that his wife is a cross that he must bear through life. Amasa accuses Dunstable of corrupting his son with his devil-magic, as Baptists are not fond of cards and tricks. Worse still is Ramsay's indoctrinating Paul into the Papistry. Amasa forbids the young Dunstable from seeing Mary and Paul any longer.

On Friday 24 October 1913 Mary Dempster goes for her last stroll about town. The town gets word that night that she has disappeared and they band together to search for her. Dunstable is allowed to help and he sees this as an affirmation of his manhood. They head for the pit, the 'local branch of hell' where kids go to give themselves up to temptation and where railway tramps abound looking for handouts. In that pit it is Dunstable who discovers Mrs. Dempster fornicating with a tramp. The townspeople catch her in the shameful act and the only defence she can offer is that 'he wanted it so badly', insinuating that this act of infidelity was sinfully consensual.

Amasa Dempster does not press charges against the tramp so he is released and warned never to return to the village. The town is abuzz about what the Reverend will say at his sermon next Sunday, and it turns out that he has chosen to resign from the parsonage and live in poverty. The wives of the community privately prohibit their husbands from expressing any public help for the disgraceful Mary Dempster, who 'had not been raped, as a decent woman would have been'. One night the townspeople paint their faces black and riot outside of the Dempster home, and Dunstable is disgusted that Amasa does not go out to face them. Amasa becomes a shell of a man and Mary is strapped up in a harness and not allowed to leave the house. Dunstable resumes his visits with Mary and Paul by sneaking in through her window while Amasa is out.

Over the next year Dunstable is ostracized at school but finds comfort and company in books. Meanwhile Leola Cruikshank is well understood to be Percy Boyd Staunton's girl. But Percy is discovered one day in a barn engaging in the sexual act with one Mabel Heighington. Percy's father pays off her family and Percy is sent away to Colbourne College, the same college that Dunstan would one day come to teach at, while Percy was Chairman of its Board of Governors.

In the autumn of 1914 war breaks out across the world, but Dunstable is more concerned with his older brother Willie's illness. Willie had been working at his father's paper when one of the rollers fell on him and damaged some internal organs. Dunstable has to stay at his brother's side while the rest of the town is at the Fall Fair, and during this sitting Willie dies. Dunstable panics but does not go for the doctor, instead he brings

Mary Dempster to the scene and she prays by Willie's bed and restores him to life. Dunstable is convinced that he has seen a miracle, but the doctor dismisses the possibility that Willie was ever dead, and Mrs. Ramsay is upset that the whore Mary Dempster is in her home.

Dunstable's friends come to view him as a 'credulous ass who thought that a dangerous lunatic could raise the dead'. Even the new Presbyterian Reverend pulls Dunstable aside to warn him against associating with women of loose virtue, and assures him that the age of miracles is past. Mrs. Ramsay will not drop the subject at home, and eventually forces her son to make a choice between her and 'that woman', and so Dunstable lies his way into being enlisted into the army. His parents will not shame him by informing the army about his true age, and so Dunstable can wait out the rest of his Deptford days in a romantic fling with Leola, who assures Dunstable that she really loves him over Percy. Dunstable also promises Mary Dempster that he will not be afraid no matter what happens.

Part Two – I Am Born Again

Ramsay is reluctant to speak about his involvement in the Great War because he admits that as an infantryman he had little idea what was going on and simply did as he was told.

He spends some two or three years at the front before November 5th, 1917 when he is injured during the Third Battle at Ypres, but not before he manages to clear a German machine gun nest by shooting three enemy soldiers in the backs of their heads. Ramsay becomes disoriented and his left leg is torn apart by shrapnel. He crawls through the mud and confusion into the remains of a building as a flare drops before him. The flare illuminates a statue of the Virgin and Child and Ramsay sees Mrs. Dempster's face in that statue as he denounces her as a fool and loses consciousness.

Ramsay is unconscious for some six months while he is being cared for at an English army hospital. He describes his unconsciousness as a blissful paradise, but his return to reality is also rather pleasant, as he is being lovingly cared for by a devoted nurse named Diana Marfleet. Ramsay had been presumed dead as his tags were lost in the battle, and he is shocked to learn that he was posthumously awarded the Victoria Cross, and less affected to learn that his parents died in the influenza pandemic of early 1918 after receiving the news that he and his brother were dead.

Ramsay is awarded his V.C. by his king, George V. Diana entices Ramsay back into life and helps him adjust to his new prosthetic leg; while also initiating him into sexual existence. She intends to marry him but when Ramsay refuses she confers upon him his new name, Dunstan, after the saint who fought off the temptations of the devil. Ramsay says that he will not marry her because doesn't want another mother-figure in his life after just having been liberated from his biological one, and also he is still receiving letters from Leola of uncertain intent.

Dunstan is treated to a hero's welcome when he returns to Deptford, and a parade is thrown in his and the other war-veterans' honour. Dunstan is surprised to find out that Percy-Boyd Staunton is a major with a D.S.O.; and very surprised when Percy announces that he and Leola are to be married. Dunstan decides to take this with good-humour and continue his friendship with the pair. Dunstan takes charge of his now emptied household and then acquaints himself with the developments of Deptford over the last four years. Doc Staunton retired from his practice when the flu epidemic struck and became a very rich man. Ramsay also learns that Amasa Dempster was felled by the flu, that Paul ran away with the circus, and that Mary went insane and was taken away by a relative. The section ends with Dunstan leaving Deptford in the flesh, though he muses that he 'never wholly left it in the spirit'.

Part Three – My Fool-Saint

Ramsay goes to school at the University of Toronto and earns an MA in History. Percy flowers brilliantly and drops his first name to become known as Boy Staunton, and he takes to modelling himself on the pinnacle of aristocratic panache: Edward, Prince of Wales. Boy studies law and plays the stock market, and is well on his way to outstripping even his father's immense accumulations of fortune. But Boy is generous to take care of his struggling and frugal friend Dunstan by providing him with investment information. They meet every two weeks so that Boy can prattle on about Leola and all the other girls he is enjoying. And Dunstan is very jealous and upset to have to hear about this, but that doesn't stop him from taking Boy's money.

After college Dunstan takes a job as a schoolmaster that he will keep until the retirement party of the second chapter of this book.

Boy and Leola are married and travel to Europe, and Dunstan visits the continent for his own amusements.

Dunstan returns to the battlefields of Europe to search for his Madonna statue. Dunstan takes up the challenge of learning the histories of all the Catholic Saints, and becomes something of an expert in the field of hagiology.

As Dunstan develops into an eccentric teacher, Boy tries to educate Leola into a higher social standing without much success. When the Prince of Wales visits Canada in 1927, Boy is selected as an aide for the Prince, and the event is possibly the greatest moment in Boy's life. A year later Boy's son is born and named Edward David Staunton.

Ramsay's school hears a guest lecture from a man named Joel Surgeoner from the Lifeline Mission to help the needy. Dunstan recognizes the man as the tramp he saw in the pit with Mary Dempster all those years ago, and follows the man to talk to him. Dunstan's mind is opened up to the possibility of illusions and parables being more real than truths, and that Mary redeemed this tramp and made him into an honest God-fearing man. Joel mentions that he considers a Saint, and Dunstan takes this as being all-too-real, and considers her redemption of Joel to be the first of three miracles she performed (the others being the resurrection of Willie, and appearing to Dunstan at Passchendaele).

Dunstan returns to Deptford one last time to gather information on the whereabouts of the insane Mary Dempster. He also stops off at the Catholic priest's house to inquire about whether or not Mary's three miracles qualify her to be a Saint. Ramsay is introduced to the concept of the 'Fool-Saint', a person full of holiness and good-will but who nonetheless brings madness.

Dunstan finds Mary in Toronto. She is being cared for by her aunt, Bertha Shanklin. The two women are not used to the company of men and Mary is not up to being reminded of the traumas in her past. Bertha allows Dunstan to come back and get to know Mary as a new friend, and not the boy from long ago.

In 1929 Boy protects Dunstan from experiencing the great depression by having him invest in Boy's own company, the Alpha Corportation, which is a sugar-refining business. At the time Dunstan is more preoccupied testing his hypotheses about the Portugese Saint Wilgefortis. He travels to a small village in Tyrolean Austria to investigate a shrine, and finds that a travelling circus, Le grand Cirque de St Vite, is in town. By an astonishing coincidence, the young magician who jumps up on stage turns out to be an older and sleazier Paul Dempster, who has obviously made a living on the trade Dunstan first schooled him in some 15 years earlier. Paul is going by the name Faustus Legrand, and is not pleased to be reminded of his former life in Canada. Dunstan returns to his investigations of Uncumber and later discovers that Paul stole his wallet.

Part Four – Gyges and King Candaules

Boy's dealings with solaces make him rich off of the Depression. Dunstan is only too thrilled to hear about Boy's successes and how Leola is getting old. It seems that Leola is unable to keep pace with Boy's rapid rise through the social ranks. Dunstan doesn't want to intervene as their marriage dissolves into enmity and claims that he feels nothing for Leola now except pity. Dunstan also reveals the strange circumstances that surrounded the night of David's conception and it seems Dunstan was a rather integral part of that process... which raises certain questions that David will investigate during The Manticore. Dunstan compares the situation between him and Boy to the story of Gyges and King Candaules, as a warning, but Boy is not the type to concern himself with archetypal patterns shaping human lives.

Dunstan reminds us that he visited Mary Dempster every fortnight for four years, until her Aunt died and Mary was left to his care. He places her in a public hospital for the insane, in Toronto, where he can keep an eye on her, and he can see that she is not happy to be there.

Dunstan achieves a specialized though limited reputation in the realm of hagiography when the Bollandists agree to publish an article of his. Dunstan travels to Europe again to meet with them, and though he knows he can never be a part of their world, he is satisfied to have achieved recognition in his chosen field of study. He makes a friend of the oldest Jesuit in the bunch, Padre Blazon, who is happy to talk at length in exchange for food and liquor. The Padre reveals the earthly lives of the saints, the side that history has repressed because of the human need for examples of excellence and things they cannot explain. Blazon also offers some advice on Dunstan's fool-saint, advancing the possibility that she saved Dunny from that rock when he was a child for a reason, and that Dunstan should figure out what role she is playing in his personal mythology.

Dunstan continues his weekly visits with Mary Dempster, but they are becoming a chore to him. Next he compiles his first book, A Hundred Saints for Travellers, which is intended for simple identification, while his next book explores why people need saints.

Dunstan becomes an eccentric friend for Boy to promote at his various social functions. In this chapter Dunstan also covers the early years of David and Caroline Staunton, along with Boy's rampant philandering. But in 1936 things take a tragic turn in the Staunton household when Boy's hero finally ascends to the throne, only to abdicate it by the end of the year. That Christmas proves to be the undoing of the Stauntons, and by the time Dunstan arrives for dinner, Boy has stormed off, Leola is crying, and the kids are traumatized for life. Leola tries to seduce Dunstan and remind him of when they were together. When Dunstan decides to leave, she screams out "You don't love me!" Dunstan flees the scene, only to be called back by one of the Staunton servants, and when Dunstan returns Leola is wrapped up in her bed after having slit her wrists and bled all over the bathroom. She had intended to kill herself but had done a poor job of it. She also left a note confessing her love for Dunstan. Dunstan is sure the nurse has read this note, and possibly told the children, but he has the unfortunate duty of helping Leola return to life as Boy has disappeared on a drinking binge and does not return for many weeks.

Themes

Davies discusses several themes in the novel, perhaps the most important being the difference between materialism and spirituality. Davies asserts religion is not necessarily integral to the idea—demonstrated by the corrupt Reverend Leadbeater who reduces the Bible to mere economic terms.

Davies, then being an avid student of Carl Jung's ideas, deploys them in *Fifth Business*. Characters are clear examples of Jungian archetypes and events demonstrate Jung's idea of synchronicity. The stone thrown at Ramsay when he was a child reappears decades later in a scandalous suicide or murder. Ramsay's character is a classic introverted personality, contrasted throughout the book with the extroverted sensuality of Boy Staunton. Ramsay dedicates his life to genuine religious feeling as he saw it in his 'fool-saint' Mary Dempster, whose son grows up to be the very archetype of The Magician.

A genuinely learned man, Davies wrote a prose that both poked fun at pretentious scholarship and enjoyed joking allusions, as in the names of Ramsay's girl friends, Agnes Day, Gloria Mundy and Libby Doe. He explained these later as "Agnes, the Sufferer — a type well known to all men; Gloria, the Good Time Girl, and Libby, the energetic go-getter."

Religion and morality

There is religious sectarianism in Deptford dividing the frontier townsfolk between five different Christian churches that do not associate with each other under normal circumstances. It takes emergency situations for them to lend aid to each other, but this is conditional aid based on the assumption that certain moral codes will be preserved regardless of faith. For instance, Mary Dempster is a daft-headed girl who habitually flouts the norms of the society, and so she finds herself ostracized and ridiculed by her society, and no one comes to her aid when her son runs away. But she is the only member of Deptford society that Dunstan views as truly 'religious' in her attitude because she lives according to a light that arises from within (which he contrasts with her husband's 'deeply religious' attitude, which 'meant that he imposed religion as he understood it on everything he knew or encountered').

As a boy, Dunstable is raised as a Presbyterian, but he also takes an avid interest in Catholic saints. He grows up to develop a more spiritual mode of life that is not reliant on external structures. For Dunstan Ramsay, religion and morality are immediate certainties in life, and the events of the novel show how moral lapses have a way of 'snowballing' and coming back to haunt one.

Myth and History

Davies and Dunstan here are at pains to illustrate to us just how fluid the concept of historical fact really is, and that it is not so distinct from the suppositions of mythic thinking. Dunstan questions the extent that he can provide an accurate of the events of his childhood or his participation in WW1 campaigns, because what he recalls is surely distinct from the 'consensually accepted reality'.

One aspect of this blurred distinction between myth and history is Ramsay's lifelong preoccupation with the lives of the Saints. The fantastic nature of their stories were always grounded in actual events, but their miracles were given attention and focus based on the psychosocial attitudes and needs of the day, so that what the public wanted had a large measure of influence over what became the accepted canon.

7

Life and Works of Michael Ondaatje

Philip Michael Ondaatje OC (born 12 September 1943) is a Sri Lankan-born Canadian novelist and poet of Colombo Chetty and Burgher origin. He is perhaps best known for his Booker Prize-winning novel, *The English Patient,* which was adapted into an Academy-Award-winning film.

Michael Ondaatje was born in Colombo, Sri Lanka (then Ceylon) of parents of Russian descent, and moved to England with his mother in 1954. After relocating to Canada in 1962, Ondaatje became a Canadian citizen. He studied for a time at Bishops College School and Bishop's University in Lennoxville, Quebec, but moved to Toronto, where he received his BA from the University of Toronto and his MA from Queen's in Kingston, Ontario. He then began teaching at the University of Western Ontario in London, Ontario. In 1970, he settled in Toronto and, from 1971 to 1988, taught English Literature there at York University and Glendon College.

Ondaatje and his wife, novelist and academic Linda Spalding, co-edit *Brick, A Literary Journal,* with Michael Redhill, Michael Helm, and Esta Spalding.

His style of fiction was introduced in *Coming Through Slaughter* (1976) and mastered in *The English Patient* (1992). He creates a narrative by exploring many interconnected snapshots in minute detail.

Although he is best known as a novelist, Ondaatje's work has also encompassed autobiography, poetry and film. A semi-fictional memoir of his Sri Lankan childhood is called *Running in the Family* (1982). He has published thirteen books of poetry, and won the Governor General's Award for two of them, namely *The Collected Works of Billy the Kid* (1970) and *There's a Trick With a Knife I'm Learning to Do: Poems 1973-1978* (1979).

The Collected Works of Billy the Kid and *Coming Through Slaughter* have been adapted for the stage and produced in numerous theatrical productions across North America. Ondaatje's three films include a documentary on fellow poet B.P. Nichol, *Sons of Captain Poetry,* and *The Clinton Special: A Film About The Farm Show,* which chronicles a collaborative theatre experience led in 1971 by Paul Thompson of Theatre Passe Muraille. In 2002, Ondaatje published a non-fiction book, *The Conversations: Walter Murch and the Art of Editing Film,* which won special recognition at the 2003 American Cinema Editors Awards, as well as a Kraszna-Krausz Book Award for best book of the year on the moving image.

Ondaatje has also, since the 1960s, been involved with Toronto's influential Coach House Books, supporting the independent small press by working as a poetry editor.

He is also known for five other works of fiction:

1. *Anil's Ghost* — winner of the 2000 Giller Prize, the Prix Médicis, the Kiriyama Pacific Rim Book Prize,

the 2001 Irish Times International Fiction Prize and Canada's Governor General's Award.

2. *The English Patient* – winner of the Booker Prize, the Canada Australia Prize, and the Canadian Governor General's Award and later made into a motion picture, winning the Academy Award for Best Picture. *The English Patient* can be considered a sequel to *In the Skin of a Lion* (1987).
3. *In the Skin of a Lion* – A fictional story about early immigrant settlers in Toronto, it is the winner of the 1988 City of Toronto Book Award, finalist for the 1987 Ritz Paris Hemingway Award for best novel of the year in English, and winner of the first Canada Reads competition in 2002.
4. *Coming Through Slaughter* – a fictional story of New Orleans, Louisiana about 1900, very loosely based on the lives of jazz pioneer Buddy Bolden and photographer E. J. Bellocq. Winner of the 1976 Books in Canada First Novel Award
5. *Divisadero* – Winner of the 2007 Governor General's Literary Award for Fiction.

In 1988, Ondaatje was made an Officer of the Order of Canada (OC) and two years later a Foreign Honorary Member of the American Academy of Arts and Letters.

He has two children and is the brother of philanthropist, businessman and author Christopher Ondaatje. His nephew David is a film director and screenwriter who made the 2009 film *The Lodger*.

8

Writings of Margaret Atwood

Margaret Eleanor Atwood, CC, O.Ont, FRSC (born November 18, 1939) is a Canadian author, poet, critic, essayist, feminist and social campaigner. She is among the most-honoured authors of fiction in recent history; she is a winner of the Arthur C. Clarke Award and Prince of Asturias award for Literature, has been shortlisted for the Booker Prize five times, winning once, and has been a finalist for the Governor General's Award seven times, winning twice. While she may be best known for her work as a novelist, she is also an award winning poet, having published 15 books of poetry to date. Many of her poems have been inspired by myths, and fairy tales, which were an interest of hers from an early age. Atwood has also published short stories in *Tamarack Review, Alphabet, Harper's, CBC Anthology, Ms., Saturday Night, Playboy,* and many other magazines.

Born in Ottawa, Ontario, Canada, Atwood is the second of three children of Margaret Dorothy (née Killam), a former dietitian and nutritionist, and Carl Edmund Atwood, an entomologist. Due to her father's ongoing research in forest entomology, Atwood spent much of her childhood in the backwoods of Northern

Quebec and back and forth between Ottawa, Sault Ste. Marie and Toronto. She did not attend school full-time until she was 11 years old. She became a voracious reader of literature, Dell pocketbook mysteries, Grimm's Fairy Tales, Canadian animal stories, and comic books. She attended Leaside High School in Leaside, Toronto and graduated in 1957.

Atwood began writing at age six and realized she wanted to write professionally when she was 16. In 1957, she began studying at Victoria University in the University of Toronto. Her professors included Jay Macpherson and Northrop Frye. She graduated in 1961 with a Bachelor of Arts in English (honours) and minors in philosophy and French.

In late 1961, after winning the E.J. Pratt Medal for her privately printed book of poems, *Double Persephone,* she began graduate studies at Harvard's Radcliffe College with a Woodrow Wilson fellowship. She obtained a master's degree (MA) from Radcliffe in 1962 and pursued further graduate studies at Harvard University for 2 years, but never finished because she never completed a dissertation on "The English Metaphysical Romance" in 1967. She has taught at the University of British Columbia (1965), Sir George Williams University in Montreal (1967-68), the University of Alberta (1969-79), York University in Toronto (1971-72), and New York University, where she was Berg Professor of English.

Critical Reception

The Economist called her a "scintillating wordsmith" and an "expert literary critic", but commented that her logic does not match her prose in *Payback: Debt and the Shadow Side of Wealth,* a book which commences with the conception of debt and its kinship with justice. Atwood claims that this conception is ingrained in the human psyche, manifest as it is in early historical peoples, who matched their conceptions of debt with those of justice as typically exemplified by a female deity. Atwood holds that, with the rise of Ancient Greece, and especially the installation of the court system detailed in Aeschylus's *Oresteia,* this deity has been replaced by a more thorough conception of debt.

In 2003, Shaftesbury Films produced an anthology series, *The Atwood Stories,* which dramatized six of Atwood's short stories.

Atwood and Science Fiction

The Handmaid's Tale received the very first Arthur C. Clarke Award for the best science fiction novel first published in the United Kingdom during the previous year, in 1987. It was also nominated for the 1986 Nebula Award, and the 1987 Prometheus Award, both science fiction awards.

Atwood was at one time offended at the suggestion that *The Handmaid's Tale* or *Oryx and Crake* were science fiction, insisting to *The Guardian* that they were speculative fiction instead: "Science fiction has monsters and spaceships; speculative fiction could really happen." She told the Book of the Month Club: "*Oryx and Crake* is a speculative fiction, not a science fiction proper. It contains no intergalactic space travel, no teleportation, no Martians." and on *BBC Breakfast* explained that science fiction, as opposed to what *she* wrote, was "talking squids in outer space." The latter phrase particularly rankled among advocates of science fiction, and frequently recurs when her writing is discussed.

Atwood has since said that she does at times write science fiction, and that *Handmaid's Tale* and *Oryx and Crake* can be designated as such. She clarified her meaning on the difference between speculative and science fiction, while admitting that others use the terms interchangeably: "For me, the science fiction label belongs on books with things in them that we can't yet do.... speculative fiction means a work that employs the means already to hand and that takes place on Planet Earth", and said that science fictional narratives give a writer the ability to explore themes in ways that realistic fiction cannot.

Contribution to the Theorizing of Canadian Identity

Atwood's contributions to the theorizing of Canadian identity have garnered attention both in Canada and internationally. Her principal work of literary criticism, *Survival: A Thematic Guide to Canadian Literature*, is considered outdated in Canada but remains the standard introduction to Canadian literature in Canadian Studies programs internationally. In *Survival*, Atwood postulates that Canadian literature, and by extension Canadian identity, is characterized by the symbol of survival. This symbol is expressed in the omnipresent use of "victim positions" in Canadian literature. These positions represent a scale of self-consciousness and self-actualization for the victim in the "victor/victim" relationship. The "victor" in these scenarios may be other humans, nature, the wilderness or other external and internal factors which oppress the victim Atwood's *Survival* bears the influence of Northrop Frye's theory of garrison mentality; Atwood instrumentalizes Frye's concept to a critical tool. More recently, Atwood has continued her exploration of the implications of Canadian literary themes for Canadian identity in lectures such as *Strange Things: The Malevolent North in Canadian Literature* (1995).

Atwood's contribution to the theorizing of Canada is not limited to her non-fiction works. Several of her works, including *The Journals of Susanna Moodie, Alias Grace, The Blind Assassin* and *Surfacing,* are examples of what postmodern literary theorist Linda Hutcheon calls "Historiographic Metafiction". In such works, Atwood explicitly explores the relation of history and narrative and the processes of creating history.

Ultimately, according to her theories in works such as *Survival* and her exploration of similar themes in her fiction, Atwood considers Canadian literature as the expression of Canadian identity. According to this literature, Canadian identity has been defined by a fear of nature, by settler history and by unquestioned adherence to the community.

Personal Life

In 1968, Atwood married Jim Polk, whom she divorced in 1973. She formed a relationship with fellow novelist Graeme Gibson soon after and moved to Alliston, Ontario, north of Toronto. In 1976 their daughter, Eleanor Jess Atwood Gibson, was born. Atwood returned to Toronto in 1980. She divides her time between Toronto and Pelee Island, Ontario.

In March 2008 it was announced by Atwood, via television hookup between Toronto and Vancouver, that she had accepted her first chamber opera commission. 'Pauline' will be on the subject of Pauline Johnson, a writer and Canadian artist long a subject of fascination to Atwood. It will star Judith Forst, with music by Christos Hatzis, and be produced by City

Opera of Vancouver. 'Pauline' will be set at Vancouver, British Columbia, in March 1913, in the last week in the life of Johnson

Political Involvement

Although Atwood's politics are commonly described as being left wing, she has indicated in interviews that she considers herself a Red Tory in the historical sense of the term. Atwood and her partner Graeme Gibson are currently members of the Green Party of Canada and strong supporters of GPC leader Elizabeth May, whom Atwood has referred to as fearless, honest, reliable and knowledgeable. In the 2008 federal election she attended a rally for the Bloc Québécois, a Quebec separatist party, because of her support for their position on the arts, and stated that she would vote for the party if she lived in Quebec. In a *Globe and Mail* editorial, she urged Canadians to vote for any other party to stop a Conservative majority.

Atwood has strong views on environmental issues, such as suggesting that gas-powered leaf blowers and lawn mowers be banned, and has made her own home more energy efficient by installing awnings and skylights that open, and by not having air-conditioning. She and her partner also use a hybrid car when they are in the city.

During the debate in 1987 over a free trade agreement between Canada and the United States, Atwood spoke out against the deal, including an essay she wrote opposing the agreement.

Atwood celebrated her 70th birthday at a gala dinner at Laurentian University in Sudbury, Ontario, marking the final stop of her international tour to promote *The Year of the Flood*. She stated that she had chosen to attend the event because the city has been home to one of Canada's most ambitious environmental reclamation programs:

> "When people ask if there's hope (for the environment), I say, if Sudbury can do it, so can you. Having been a symbol of desolation, it's become a symbol of hope."

Surfacing

Surfacing is the second published novel by Canadian author Margaret Atwood. It was first published by McClelland and Stewart in 1972. It has been called a companion novel to Atwood's collection of poems, Power Politics, which was written the previous year and deals with complementary issues. The novel, grappling with notions of national and gendered identity, anticipated rising concerns about conservation and preservation and the emergence of Canadian nationalism. It was adapted into a movie in 1981.

Plot

The book tells the story of a woman who returns to her hometown in Canada to find her missing father. Accompanied by her lover and another married couple, the unnamed protagonist meets her past in her childhood house, recalling events and feelings, while trying to find clues for her father's mysterious disappearance. Little by little, the past overtakes her and drives her into the realm of wildness and madness.

Themes

Separation

Separation is a major theme of Surfacing. This is

established in the first chapter, when the narrator is shown to be politically dispossessed as an English-speaker in Quebec, at a time in which Quebec was aspiring to become an independent French-speaking nation. The narrator also feels disconnected from the people around her, equating human interaction with that of animals. For example, while overhearing David and Anna make love, the narrator thinks "of an animal at the moment the trap closes".

The mouthpiece for feelings of nationalism is extremist David, who claims Canada would be better without the "fascist pig Yanks" and suggests they be driven from the country by attack beavers.

Madness

Another theme is madness. The protagonist's mental reasoning deteriorates sharply, as the story unfolds from initial signs of mental health issues to a full-blown psychosis. Because Atwood has written in the first person, we are told much of the narrative through monologues, and experience events through the thoughts of the protagonist. This allows for a very detailed and personal portrayal of a mind 'undoing itself'. Although there are nuances in the protagonist's thoughts that suggest mental problems in early chapters, the narrative takes a decisive plunge on page 67. At this point we learn that the protagonist has had a severe trauma in her early adult life, as she sits trying to piece together her past: "then static, like a jumped track". This discovery that she is unable to identify any strong narrative themes in her own memories causes her substantial worry. She finds that she cannot trust her own thoughts, for instance she interrupts her own thinking with a retort: "That's a lie..." This inability to 'know which is the right thought' is profoundly psychotic and from that point on the narrative and the thought processes of the protagonist become disturbingly uncoordinated. She has false memories of her father as a werewolf and her mother feeding jays: the intersection of fairy tales with daily life demonstrate the fragmentation of the narrator's mind.

Feminism

Feminism, a theme in many of Atwood's novels, is explored through the perspective of the female narrative, exposing the ways women are marginalized in their professional and private lives.

Language and the Return to Nature

Atwood's protagonist is never named in the novel and is therefore often referred to by critics as "the surfacer". The character undergoes a significant metamorphosis during the novel and apparently seeks to discard her identity as a human and to assume that of an animal. The surfacer travels with her partner, Joe, and another couple, David and Anna; journeying from the city into the wilderness in which she grew up. Whilst the trip is ostensibly undertaken in order for the surfacer to investigate the disappearance of her father, it is clear that her reasons are in fact even more personal, and not yet obvious even to her.

Throughout the novel, the surfacer reveals a deep-seated distrust of language, which she refers to as being something she "couldn't use because it wasn't mine". Furthermore, she reveals her attitude to language when she asserts that "[i]f you look like them and talk like them and think like them then you are them [...] you speak their language, a language is everything you do" – she is talking, ostensibly, about Americans, but the sentiment may equally be applied to all of humanity. Only humans use language so to discard your humanity you must discard your language. Unfortunately, this reasoning seems to be flawed. In reality, language is the means by which humans seek to describe and make sense of their environment. It has been argued that, outside of language, there is literally nothing – no environment. Whilst it would be an exaggeration to say that our entire understanding of the world is derived from language, it is nevertheless the most important means by which we derive the largest part of our understanding.

Language, to the surfacer, often appears alien. When refusing to have sex with Anna's partner, David, for instance, she searches for "a vocabulary that would work" in order to deter him. It is clear that the use of language is not entirely natural to her. This may be explained, partly, by the fact that she has grown up in rural Canada, in an area in which both the English and French languages are spoken. As an exclusively English speaker, the surfacer "discovered people could say words that would go into my ears meaning nothing".

This could go some way towards explaining why the character appears to have difficulty in reconciling herself with her world. She apparently lacks, or at least sees the limitations of, the vital school of language. The surfacer seems to realise that language is not an effective tool in the her quest, and appears to conclude that the best way to comprehend nature is to abandon language altogether, and become more animal-like.

Atwood's protagonist therefore seeks enlightenment through some kind of closer and more direct communication with - or submergence into - the natural world.

As the surfacer begins to dispense with language, regarding it as a barrier to understanding, it appears that she attempts to break down the barrier between words and objects, asserting that "the animals learned to eat without nouns" and "the animals have no need for speech, why talk when you are a word?". This is the clearest indication that she now sees no distinction between words and objects.

Christian theology holds that, at the time of the creation, there was indeed no separation between objects and their signifiers. The word literally – in every sense – was the object and the two were inseparable, thus the book of John tells us that "In the beginning was the Word, and the Word was with God, and the Word was God". It is only after humanity's fall from grace in the garden of Eden that the two become separated.

In effect, humans are separated from a deep understanding of the world by language. It seems, however, that the surfacer seeks to gain enlightenment by reuniting the two, or at least by disregarding their separation, and returning to an animal-like state.

The surfacer seems to feel the wilderness beginning to inhabit her: "the creature in me, plant-animal, sends out filaments in me". This passage is highly reminiscent of another Atwood piece, the poem 'Departure from the Bush', from The Journals of Susanna Moodie, in which the central character comes to belong to her environment and is said to be "crept in upon by green". However, the transformation of the

Susanna Moodie character takes place slowly, and in an unforced way, over a period of years, whereas the surfacer seems to be making a conscious attempt to metamorphosise, and whereas the Moodie character's transformation, controlled by nature, appears welcome and successful, the surfacer's forced metamorphosis is less so.

Prior to her transformation, it becomes clear that Atwood's protagonist is, in fact, trying to come to terms with an earlier decision to abort her unborn child. She begins to believe, however, that nothing truly dies, and that death is simply a part of life, and that death fuels life: ""I remember the heron; by now it will be insects, frogs, fish, other herons." Rather than see the heron as dead, she regards it as being alive: transferred to the other creatures that it has fed, and she appears to seek such a transformation for herself. She also refuses to accept the death of her father, and later meets, apparently, his spirit. "I see now that although it isn't my father it is what my father has become. I knew he wasn't dead". It is clear that, through her own metamorphosis, the surfacer seeks to overcome death, for the sake of her aborted baby.

The surfacer insists that she and Joe go outside to have sex, saying that inside is "not the place". She imagines him, and herself, as animals. He "unzips his human skin", but "needs to grow fur", whilst she uses her "tentacled feet and free hand [to] scent out the way". As they have sex ("it's the right season") she feels her lost child is "forgiving" her. She knows she will become pregnant, and imagines giving birth in an animalesque way, "licking blood from the cord the blood returning to the ground as it is supposed to" She now abandons her human existence and imagines she will "grow fur on my skin". However, the conception of a new baby seems to offer healing. The surfacer has gone through a cycle of grief, and eventually arrives at the final stage: acceptance.

9

Literary Life of Ralph Connor

Rev. Dr. Charles William Gordon, or Ralph Connor, (September 13, 1860 - October 31, 1937) was a Canadian novelist, using the Connor pen name while maintaining his status as a Church leader, first in the Presbyterian and later the United churches in Canada. Gordon was also at one time a master at Upper Canada College. He sold more than five million copies of his works in his lifetime, and some of his works are still in print.

Gordon was born in Glengarry County, Ontario, the son of Rev. Daniel Gordon (1822–1910) and Mary Robertson Gordon (d. 1890). His father was a Free Church of Scotland Missionary in Upper Canada. The family moved from Glengarry to Harrington, Oxford County, Ontario when he was a youth. Like many other young men in the area, Gordon went to Toronto to study at University of Toronto. He then attended Knox College and graduated with distinction in 1886.

Ministerial Career

With a brother and two Knox College classmates he travelled to Scotland and Europe and spent a term of study in Edinburgh. He was ordained a Presbyterian misinster in 1890. He moved to Alberta, then still part of the Northwest Territories, and he served a large area west of Calgary that today includes the municipalities of Banff and Canmore. He served in the Rocky Mountains until 1894. The congregation in Canmore is called Ralph Connor Memorial United Church in rembrance of his time there.

He moved to Winnipeg, Manitoba where he would spend nearly 40 years as minister of St. Stephen's Presbyterian/United Church, which was a new congregation when he arrived. During these 40 years he also wrote in Kenora, Ontario on Lake of the Woods.

Near the start of the First World War, in 1915 he became Chaplain of the 43rd (Cameron Highlanders) Battalion CEF. In 1916 he was made senior chaplain of Canadian Forces in England with the rank of Major. He then proceeded to France as senior chaplain, 9th Brigade, British Expeditionary Force. He was mentioned in Imperial despatches.

After returning from Europe, he was Moderator of the 1921 Presbyterian General Assembly and became a strong advocate for union of the Presbyterian, Methodist and Congregational Churches in Canada. In June 1925, he was on the podium during the final benediction of the Presbyterian Church General Assembly at Toronto's College Street Church. He encouraged the organist to play Handel's Hallelujah Chorus as loudly as possible to drown out the sound of protests from the so-called "Continuing Presbyterians" who had gathered in the front corner of the assembly hall to vote on resuming nearby later that evening.

Writing Career

Gordon became interested in writing during his student days at the University of Toronto. He published his first novel, *Black Rock*, in 1898. While the book was moderately successful in Canada, his second novel, *The Sky Pilot*, gained him international attention in 1899 and sold more than 1,000,000 copies. *The Sky Pilot*, like many of his works, was a frontier adventure with strong themes of morality and justice. He continued to write until his death in 1937. His autobiography, *Postscript to Adventure* was penned in his final year and published posthumously in 1938.

Ralph Connor House

Ralph Connor House is a Canadian, Manitoba and Winnipeg heritage treasure. The home was not only built to accommodate the Gordon's large family, but also served as the St. Stephen's parish office for the Presbyterian minister.

From humble parishioners to Hollywood movie stars, the home welcomed people from all over the world, attracted to Reverend Gordon who had gained international acclaim for his good works and stardom as one of the world's best selling novelists of the time.

While Reverend Gordon's writing had made him a wealthy man in the early part of the 20th century, the Great Depression and financial problems had taken their toll and the family was forced to surrender the House to the City of Winnipeg. In 1939, the University Women's Club saved the vacant Ralph Connor House from demolition and eventually bought it from the City in 1945. The Club continued its focus on intellectual pursuits and community activity. It has been the most ardent and long-term participant in its preservation. In 1949, the Club established the Ralph Connor Trust Fund to provide for building maintenance and repairs. The Fund has spent $400,000 since 1981 to maintain and repair the House, including foundation underpinnings and new copper plumbing. But the fund was not designed to cover the scale of work now required to meet present-day fire and safety regulations and other needed functional improvements.

The Friends of Ralph Connor House was established in 2003 as a registered charity and became the official owner of the House with a focus on the care and preservation of the building.

Publications

In 1972, the National Library of Canada released *The Works of Ralph Connor* which listed some 43 titles as well as three books for which he wrote the introductions. His publications include:

1. *The angel and the star*. Toronto, Revell, 1908. 63p.
2. *The arm of gold*. Toronto, McClelland and Stewart, 1932. 314p.
3. *Beyond the marshes*. Toronto, Westminster, 1898. 36p.
4. *Black Rock, a tale of the Selkirks*. Toronto, Westminster, 1898. 327 p.
5. *Breaking the record*. New York, Revell, 1904. 31p.
6. *The Man from Glengarry*
7. *Glengarry School Days*

Legacy

Gordon United Church, founded in 1956 in Victoria, British Columbia, was named in his honour. Charles Gordon Sr. Public School in Scarborough, Ontario was also named after him. At his death Connor/Gordon left his wife and seven children. Among the latter were Professor King Gordon of Montreal, Mrs. Humphrey Carver of Toronto, Mrs. Arthur B. Brown of Toronto, Lois Gordon of Montreal and Allison and Ruth Gordon of Winnipeg. Some of his books, including *Black Rock, The Man from Glengarry* and *Glengarry School Days* are still in print.

10

Writings of Thomas B. Costain

Bertram Costain (May 8, 1885 - October 8, 1965) was a Canadian journalist who became a best-selling author of historical novels at the age of 57. Costain was born in Brantford, Ontario to John Herbert Costain and Mary Schultz. He attended high school there as well as the Brantford Collegiate Institute. Before graduating from high school he had written four novels, one of which was a 70,000 word romance about Maurice of Nassau, Prince of Orange. These early novels were all rejected by publishers.

Costain's career as a writer began in 1902 when the Brantford Courier accepted a mystery story from him, and he became a reporter there (for five dollars a week). He was an editor at the Guelph *Daily Mercury* between 1908 and 1910. He married Ida Randolph Spragge (1888-1975) in York, Ontario on January 12, 1910. The couple had two children, Molly (Mrs. Howard Haycraft) and Dora (Mrs. Henry Darlington Steinmetz). Also in 1910, Costain joined the Maclean Publishing Group where he edited three trade journals. Beginning in 1914, he was a staff writer for and, from 1917, editor of Toronto-based *Maclean's* magazine. His success there brought him to the attention of *The*

Saturday Evening Post in New York City where he was fiction editor for fourteen years.

In 1920 he became a naturalized U.S. citizen. He also worked for Doubleday Books as an editor 1939-1946. He was the head of 20th Century Fox's bureau of literary development (story department) from 1934 to 1942.

In 1940, he wrote four short novels but was "enough of an editor not to send them out". He next turned to a plan to write six books in a series he called "The Stepchildren of History". He would write about six interesting but unknown historical figures. For his first, he wrote about the seventeenth century pirate John Ward aka Jack Ward.

In 1942, he realized his longtime dream when this first novel *For My Great Folly* was published, and it became a bestseller with over 132,000 copies sold The *New York Times* reviewer stated at the end of the review "there will be no romantic-adventure lover left unsatisfied." In January 1946 he "retired" to spend the rest of his life writing, at a rate of about 3,000 words a day.

Raised as a Baptist, he was reported in the 1953 *Current Biography* to be an attendant of the Protestant Episcopal Church. He was described as a handsome, tall, broad-shouldered man with a pink and white complexion, clear blue eyes, and a slight Canadian accent. He was white-haired by the time he began to write novels. He loved animals and could not even kill a bug (but he also loved bridge, and he did not extend the same policy to his partners). He also loved movies and the theatre (he met his future wife when she was performing Ruth in the *The Pirates of Penzance*).

Costain's work is a mixture of commercial history (such as *The White and The Gold,* a history of New France to around 1720) and fiction that relies heavily on historic events (one review stated it was hard to tell where history leaves off and apocrypha begins). His most popular novel was *The Black Rose* (1945), centered in the time and actions of Bayan of the Baarin also known as Bayan of the Hundred Eyes. Costain noted in his forward that he initially intended the book to be about Bayan and Edward I, but became caught up in the legend of Thomas a Becket's parents: an English knight married to an Eastern girl. The book was a selection of the Literary Guild with a first printing of 650,000 copies and sold over two million copies in its first year.

His research led him to believe that Richard III was a great monarch tarred by conspiracies, after his death, with the murder of the princes in the tower. Costain supported his theories with documentation, suggesting that the real murderer was Henry VII.

Costain died in 1965 at his New York City home of a heart attack at the age of 80. He is buried in the Farringdon Cemetery in Brantford.

The Black Rose

The Black Rose is a 1950 20th Century-Fox film starring Tyrone Power and Orson Welles, loosely based on Thomas B. Costain's book. It was filmed partly on location in England and Morocco which substitutes for the Gobi Desert of China. The film was partly conceived as a follow-up to the movie *Prince of Foxes,* and reunited the earlier film's two stars. Talbot Jennings' screenplay was based on a popular novel of the same name by Canadian author Thomas B. Costain, published in 1945.

The story concerns 13th-century Saxon nobleman Walter of Gurnie (Tyrone Power), who, after sparking an unsuccessful rebellion against the Norman conquerors of his homeland, sets out to seek his fortune in the Far East. In the company of his friend Tristam (Jack Hawkins), Walter makes the acquaintance of megalomaniac Mongol warlord Bayan (Orson Welles). The "Black Rose" of the title is the beauteous Maryam (Cécile Aubry), with whom Walter fell in love while both were prisoners of Bayan.

Journeying farther east, Walter and Tristam arrive in China, where they are treated with deference - so long as they never try to leave. Eventually escaping his Chinese hosts, Walter returns to his native country. Previously denounced by King Edward (Michael Rennie) because of his role in the a Saxon rebellion, Walter is welcomed back with open arms because of all the cultural and scientific wonders (including gunpowder) he has brought back from China.

The Silver Chalice

The Silver Chalice is a 1952 English language historical novel by Thomas B. Costain. It is the fictional story of the making of a silver chalice to hold the Holy Grail and includes first century biblical and historical figures: Luke, Joseph of Arimathea, Simon Magus and his companion Helena, and the apostle Peter.

The story was inspired by the archeological discovery of a first century silver chalice in Antioch. It is in effect a prequel to the Arthurian Legend, where the search for the Holy Grail plays a conspicuous part.

Two years after its publication, Warner Bros. released a feature adaptation of the book. The film starred Paul Newman, in his first studio role, as Basil the craftsman.

First published in 1952, this classic recounts the story of Basil, a young silversmith, who is commissioned by the apostle Luke to fashion a holder for the cup Jesus used at the Last Supper.

The Silver Chalice was a top best-selling fiction title of 1953 in the United States, atop the New York Times Best Seiler List from September 7, 1952 to March 8, 1953, and remaining 64 weeks on the list until October 25, 1953.

The Silver Chalice takes place in Israel and other parts of the Roman Empire shortly after the death of Jesus. A young man, Basil, is adopted by a rich man, but loses his fortune when his father dies and his uncle defrauds him claiming he was purchased as a slave and sells him. As a slave he survives by working as an artist and silversmith. He gains his freedom, becomes a Christian and is commissioned to create an outer covering for the cup Jesus drank from at The Last Supper.

The plot of The Silver Chalice centers on the Grail—the cup from which Christ drank at the Last Supper. Tired of "all the Arthurian tripe about the Holy Grail," Costain imagined his own version of the story. Joseph of Arimathea hires Basil of Antioch, a lowborn artisan, to fashion a beautiful silver casing to hold the plain original cup that Jesus used. The casing is to be decorated with the faces of Jesus and the twelve apostles. To fulfill the commission, Basil travels throughout the ancient Mediterranean world to meet these men and those who knew them intimately.

11

Works of Bruce Barber

Bruce Barber (born in New Zealand) is an artist, writer, curator, and educator based in Halifax, Nova Scotia, where he teaches at NSCAD University. His artwork has been shown at the Paris Biennale, the Sydney Biennial, the New Museum of Contemporary Art, the Walter Phillips Gallery, London Regional Gallery, and ArtSpace Auckland. Barber is the editor of *Essays on Performance and Cultural Politicization* and of *Conceptual Art: the NSCAD Connection 1967-1973*. He is co-editor, with Serge Guilbaut and John O'Brian of *Voices of Fire: Art Rage, Power, and the State*. His critical essays have appeared in numerous anthologies, journals and magazines. His art practice is documented in the publication *Reading Rooms*. He is best known for his early performance work, his Reading Rooms, Squat Projects and his writing and theory on Littoral Art.

In his *Reading Rooms,* Barber worked with Alexander Rodchenko's 1925 Reading Room as a model for a workers' library and study. These multi-part installations made use of multi-media formats to re-present various forms of corporate advertising and news reporting. The Red Room addressed the construction of masculinity through media representation. The imagery used for critical readings was obtained from various sites of popular culture including film, advertising, war history, weapons magazines and comic books. The *Newsroom* section contained newspaper accounts of male violence; the *Viewsroom* contained slide projections; the *Videoroom* contained video footage of x-rated films and a Marvin cartoon satirising male parenting bahaviour; the *Theory/Criticism Room* provided tools with which readers could alter a selection of magazines.

A theoretical essay titled "Excision, Detournement and Reading the Open Text" elaborated the process they would have then been using. Among some of the aphorisms contained in this essay are the following:

1. The excision is less a surgical operation than a cognitive procedure, opening up the possibilities for renegotiating the areas of signification both within and beyond the image or text. Excising elements from the image confirms the existence of a primary context, pretexts and within the image itself, subtexts which disclose the competing economies of the sign(s).

2. Warning: Excision should not become the servant of censorship.

3. Close reading has never been a good substitute for criticism.

4. Absence only becomes a problem where power is concerned. Absence is difference (Jacques Derrida). Open reading allows readers to acknowledge the provisionality of meaning. Power and political efficacy is a function of use. In this

context history may represent change yet remain the same.

5. The open reader accepts his/her status as a political subject with all this may imply.
6. Open reading may assist the promotion of critical education.
7. Critical education may become education for criticism.

Operative Art

In a number of texts, beginning in the early 1980s, Barber has considered the potential for performance work to avoid its ossification into a genre category. Clearly, the type of conceptual performance art that was common in the late sixties and early seventies had run its course.

While emerging forms of postmodern performance were appropriating mainstream forms of entertainment, their critical function was often weakened or altogether abandoned. Performance could possibly withstand becoming affirmative culture (Herbert Marcuse) by rediscovering its sources in avant-garde theatre. Bertolt Brecht, for instance, echoed Karl Marx's critique of philosophy when he wrote: "The theatre became an affair for philosophers, but only for those philosophers as wished not just to explain the world, but also to change it."

Brecht coined the term *umfunctionierung* (functional transformation) to enable theatre to become an instrument to serve the interests of class struggle. And in his famous essay, "The Author as Producer," Walter Benjamin extolled the virtues of the "operative" artist, providing as his example the communist author

Sergei Tretyakov, who thought of his work not merely as descriptive reporting on reality, but an active intervention.

Benjamin believed that cultural practice should refuse modish commerce and should give work a revolutionary use value. This meant the avoidance of the impulse to aestheticize and the ordination of critical agency as a post-aesthetic strategy, one that can contain values that are nominally subsumed under several progressive political/aesthetic ideologies. In an implicit effort to politicize advanced forms of performance, Barber placed the term performance under erasure with the formulation of [performance].

Since the publication of "Towards and Adequate Interventionist [Performance] Practice" (1985), Barber has explored the radical potential of performance. The table of binary oppositions below represents general differences between two types of political action, configured as acts of protest or resistance. Depending on the circumstances and the type of event, intervention can become an exemplary action, and thus devolve into a form of political posturing, closely implicated in extreme versions of behaviour characterized by violence, anarchic rejection or destructive nihilism.

While exemplary actions are usually without theoretical support, interventions attempt to put theory into action. The intentions and ultimately the audience response are different. The exemplary action consists, instead of intervening in an overall way, in acting in a much more concentrated way on exemplary objectives, on a few key objectives that will play a determining role in the continuation of the struggle.

Among the artists that Barber has recognized for their contributions to [performance] practice - Martha Rosler, Adrian Piper, Guerrilla Art Action Group, Critical Art Ensemble and WochenKlausur, among others - he gave a priviled role to the Situationist International as an exemplary model of operative art. The SI and the students they influenced participated in occupations, sit-ins, teach-ins, theatrical agit-prop events and other forms of protest.

The SI endorsed the fundamental importance of intervention as a post-theoretical and practical aspect of their critique of the "Society of the Spectacle" - as theorized by Guy Debord. Among the theoretically informed strategies that were developed by the SI is the constructed situation. The constructed situation is bound to be collective both in its inception and development. However, it seems that at least during an initial experimental period, responsibility must fall on one particular individual.

This individual must, so to speak, be the 'director' of the situation. For example, in terms of one particular situationist project - revolving around the meeting of several friends one evening - one would expect (a) an initial period of research by the team, (b) the election of a director responsible for co-ordinating the basic elements for the construction of the decor, and for working out a number of interventions, (c) the actual people living the situation who have taken part in the whole project both theoretically and practically, and (d) a few passive spectators not knowing what the hell is going on should be reduced to action.

Communicative Action and Littoral Art

According to Barber, communicative action is very

different from direct action or intervention, although it may seem to employ some of the characteristics of both. Jürgen Habermas, who has arguably done more than anyone else to theorise various forms of political action within the public sphere, distinguishes between strategic, instrumental and communicative actions.

The distinction, he argues, between actions that are oriented toward success and those toward understanding is crucial. In strategic actions one actor seeks to influence the bahaviour of another by means of the threat of sanctions or the prospect of gratification in order to cause the interaction to continue as the first actor desires. Whereas in a communicative action one actor seeks rationally to motivate another by relying on the illocutionary binding/bonding effect of the offer contained in the speech act (J.L. Austin). Donative and Littoral art practices work in a way that challennges the strategies of the postmodern era: taking, quoting, and appropriating.

In a number of essays on "littoral art," Barber has emphasized donative art practices as examples of communicative action. Donative art actions insist that giving can be used strategically to further a number of identifiable lifeworld and humanitarian goals, as well as provide some critical intervention into the ideological fabric of our culture. While donative practices may activate a cycle of reciprocity, gifts may remain unreciprocated. Each cultural intervention, exemplary or not, engages a "logic of practice" (Pierre Bourdieu) that encourages an infinite variety of exchanges or gifts, challenges, ripostes, reciprocations, and repressions. The logic of practice privileges agency in its unpredictability and provides, according to

Habermas, an alternative to money and power as a basis for societal integration.

These sentences were written by Barber in 1998. Paragraphs on Littoral Art can be found on the Squat Official Site

1. Littoral art describes the intermediary and shifting zones between the sea and the land and refers metaphorically to cultural projects that are undertaken predominantly outside of the conventional contexts of the institutionalised artworld.
2. Littoral projects are lifeworld affirming as opposed to system reproducing. Littoral artists work between the private realm and the public sphere.
3. Littoral artists recognise their position as political subjects and act accordingly.
4. Social actions may (re)produce cultural judgments.
5. Cultural interventions may lead toward social change.
6. Public, community based art is essentially political.
7. The political positions that artists adopt should be followed ethically.
8. Littoral artists acknowledge Marx's injunction in his 11th Thesis on Feuerbach that it is not up to "philosophers (artists) to simply interpret (represent) the world; the point is to change it."
9. In Littoral art projects social interactions should be co-ordinated with less emphasis on egocentric calcultions of success for each individual and more through co-operative achievements of understanding among participants.

10. Social and cultural actions can be strategic, exemplary, instrumental or communicative. Communicative actions attempt to lessen provocation and encourage dialogue. They are the result of the conjoining of theory and practice into a political praxis.
11. In Littoral art projects no one individual should assume absolute control of the communicative process; rather it should be, in the best sense possible, participatory and democratic.
12. Public art projects are aimed at stimulating dialogue and participation within a specific community to engender (or engineer) conscientization, and possibly, social change.
13. The interaction between marginal groups, and their integration in such projects, can lead to extraordinary results in which artistic, social and environmental objectives overlap.
14. Littoral art helps to stimulate dialogue and elevate the standards of conversation between different communities and disciplines whose paths would normally not cross.
15. The littoral artist may use any form and employ any materials, techniques or procedures to reach his/her objectives.
16. Littoral art is more about giving than taking.
17. Within littoralist art practice, donative art strategies extend the language of the altruistic gift into a more politically efficacious education about the nature of giving and reciprocity.
18. Littoral artists acknowledge their debt to history and respond positively to successful models

presented by the historical avant-gardes and neo-avant-gardes of the more recent past.

19. Littoral art projects can provide a powerful incentive for social integration as opposed to individual competition.
20. Littoral art can provide an alternative to capital accumulation and power as an indicator of success.
21. Political correctness cannot rescue a bad idea. It is difficult to subvert a politically correct position.
22. Littoral projects may become art if they are concerned with art and enter the fields of discourse associated with art theory and criticism.
23. Some successful littoral projects may begin from a position of naivete.
24. Surveillance is a form of control. Observational techniques represent methods of social control.
25. Littoral artists should attempt to understand the effects of their actions and interventions in the public sphere and learn from their mistakes.
26. Artists may perceive the littoralist projects of others to be better than their own, but they should strive to approxiamte success at every level of their social engagement.
27. Littoral projects may engage directly with an institution.
28. Once the immediate objectives of the project are established, the course of events should be allowed to unfold organically. There may be many side effects that the artist cannot imagine or control. These may be used to stimulate and/or assist the development of new work.

29. The process is social and should not be tampered with. It should run its course.
30. There are many elements involved in a littoralist project. The most important may not be the most obvious.
31. If the artist uses the same methodology in a group of projects but changes the techniques and materials, one would assume that the artist's work privileged the method.
32. Banal ideas cannot be rescued by privileging the aesthetic values that may reside in the work.
33. It is difficult to bungle a good littoral project.
34. When an artist displays his/her craft too well, it may result in the loss of the social importance of the work.
35. These sentences comment on littoral art but are not art.

12

Writings of Pierre Berton

Pierre Francis de Marigny Berton, (July 12, 1920-November 30, 2004) was a noted Canadian author of non-fiction, especially Canadiana and Canadian history, and was a well-known television personality and journalist.

An accomplished storyteller, Berton was one of Canada's most prolific and popular authors. He wrote 50 books, including ones on popular culture, Canadian history, critiques of mainstream religion, anthologies, children's books and historical works for youth. He popularized Canadian history.

He was born on July 12, 1920, in Whitehorse, Yukon, where his father had moved for the 1898 Klondike Gold Rush. His family moved to Dawson City, Yukon in 1921, where they lived until moving to Victoria, British Columbia in 1932. His mother, Laura Beatrice Berton (née Thompson) was a school teacher in Toronto until she was offered a job as a teacher in Dawson City at the age of 29 in 1907. She met Frank Berton in the nearby mining town of Granville shortly after settling in Dawson and teaching kindergarten. Laura Beatrice Berton's autobiography of life in the Yukon entitled *I Married the Klondike* was published in her later years and gave her, what her son Pierre describes as 'a modicum of fame, which she thoroughly enjoyed.'

Like his father, Pierre Berton worked in Klondike mining camps during his years as a history major at the University of British Columbia, where he also worked on the student paper *The Ubyssey*. He spent his early newspaper career in Vancouver, where at 21 he was the youngest city editor on any Canadian daily, replacing editorial staff that had been called up during the Second World War.

Berton himself was conscripted into the Canadian Army under the National Resources Mobilization Act in 1942 and attended basic training in British Columbia, nominally as a reinforcement soldier intended for The Seaforth Highlanders of Canada. He elected to "go Active" (the euphemism for volunteering for overseas service) and his aptitude was such that he was appointed Lance Corporal and attended NCO school, and became a basic training instructor in the rank of corporal. Due to a background in university COTC and inspired by other citizen-soldiers who had been commissioned, he sought training as an officer.

Berton spent the next several years attending a variety of military courses, becoming, in his words, the most highly trained officer in the military. He was warned for overseas duty many times, and was granted embarkation leave many times, each time finding his overseas draft being cancelled. A coveted trainee slot with the Canadian Intelligence Corps saw Berton, now a Captain, trained to act as an Intelligence Officer (IO), and after a stint as an instructor at the Royal Military College in Kingston, Ontario, he finally went overseas in March 1945. In the UK, he was told that he would have to requalify as an IO because the syllabus in the UK was different from that in the intelligence school in Canada. By the time Berton had requalified, the war in Europe had ended. He volunteered for the Canadian Army Pacific Force (CAPF), granted a final "embarkation leave", and found himself no closer to combat employment by the time the Japanese surrendered in September 1945.

Berton moved to Toronto in 1947. At the age of 31 he was named managing editor of *Macleans*. In 1957, he became a key member of the CBC's public affairs flagship program, Close-Up, and a permanent panelist on the popular television show *Front Page Challenge*. That same year, he also narrated the Academy Award-nominated National Film Board of Canada documentary *City of Gold*, exploring life in his hometown of Dawson City during the Klondike Gold Rush. He then released an album in conjunction with Folkways Records, entitled *The Story of the Klondike: Stampede for Gold - The Golden Trail.*

Berton joined the *Toronto Star* as associate editor and columnist in 1958, leaving in 1962 to commence *The Pierre Berton Show*, which ran until 1973. It was on this show that in 1971 Berton interviewed Bruce Lee in what was to be the famous martial artist's only television interview. Berton's television career included spots as host and writer on *My Country, The Great Debate, Heritage Theatre, The Secret of My Success* and *The National Dream.*

Berton served as the Chancellor of Yukon College and, along with numerous honorary degrees, received over 30 literary awards such as the Governor General's Award for Creative Non-Fiction (three times), the

Stephen Leacock Medal of Humour, and the Gabrielle Léger Award for Lifetime Achievement in Heritage Conservation. He is a member of Canada's Walk of Fame, having been inducted in 1998. In The Greatest Canadian project, he was voted #31 in the list of great Canadians.

In 2004, Berton published his 50th book, *Prisoners of the North,* after which he announced in an interview with CanWest News Service that he was retiring from writing. On October 17, 2004, the $12.6 million Pierre Berton Resource Library, named in his honour, was opened in Vaughan, Ontario. He had lived in nearby Kleinburg, Ontario, for about fifty years.

Berton raised eyebrows in October 2004 by discussing his forty years of recreational use of marijuana on two CBC Television programs, *Play* and *Rick Mercer Report* where he openly gave tips on how to roll a joint and ended with a quick shot of him eating snacks, à la munchies.

Berton died at Sunnybrook hospital in Toronto, reportedly of heart failure, at the age of 84 on November 30, 2004.

His childhood home in Dawson City, now called Berton House, is a writers' retreat. Established writers apply for three-month long subsidized residencies there; while in residence, they give a public reading in both Dawson City and Whitehorse. The Berton House Retreat is sponsored by a charitable foundation set up to support it and by the Klondike Visitors Association; the administrator is Elsa Franklin. Franklin was Berton's long-time editor and agent.

Pierre Berton Award

Established in 1994, the Pierre Berton Award is

presented annually by Canada's National History Society for distinguished achievement in presenting Canadian history in an informative and engaging manner. Berton was the first recipient and agreed to lend his name to future awards.

13

Writings of Jeannette Armstrong

Jeannette Armstrong (born 1948) is an Okanagan Canadian author, educator, artist, and activist. She was born and grew up on the Penticton Indian reserve in British Columbia's Okanagan Valley. Armstrong has lived on the Penticton Indian Reserve for most of her life and has raised her two children there.

Armstrong's 1985 work *Slash* is considered the first novel by a Native woman in Canada. Armstrong is the grandniece of Mourning Dove, who is regarded as one of the earliest Native American woman novelists for her 1927 work *Cogewea, the Half-Blood*..

Armstrong is best known for her involvement with the En'owkin Centre, writing, and perspectives on subjects such as creativity, education, ecology, and Indigenous rights.

Early Life and Education

While growing up on the Penticton Indian Reserve, Armstrong received a formal education at a one-room school on the reserve as well as a traditional Okanagan education from her family and Elders. Armstrong's customary education enabled her to learn the Okanagan language and she remains a fluent speaker of both Okanagan and English today. For many years since her childhood, Armstrong has studied traditional Okanagan teachings and practiced traditional ways under the direction of Elders.

Armstrong first discovered her talent for and attraction to writing at age fifteen when a poem she wrote on John F. Kennedy was published in a local newspaper. As a teenager, Armstrong continued to publish poetry and develop her literary voice by listening to and reading works by Aboriginal authors such as Pauline Johnson and Chief Dan George, who she identifies as her early influences.

In 1978, Armstrong received a diploma of Fine Arts from Okanagan College and a Bachelor of Fine Arts degree from the University of Victoria where she studied Creative Writing. Armstrong's education establishes the basis for her multifarious work and accomplishments.

Armstrong as Educator

In 1978 Jeannette Armstrong began employment with the Penticton Band in a number of cultural and political capacities while also pursuing her work as a researcher, consultant, and writer at the En'owkin Centre.

The En'owkin Centre, located on the Penticton Indian Reserve and operated exclusively by the six bands of the Okanagan Nation, is managed in conjunction with Okanagan College and the University of Victoria and aims to provide students with a strong cultural and academic foundation for success in further post-secondary studies. The objectives of the society which governs En'owkin, as Armstrong describes, are "to record and perpetuate and promote 'Native' in the cultural sense, in education, and in our lives and our communities"

To support these objectives, the En'owkin Centre created the Okanagan Curriculum Project as a component of its institution. This project aspires to develop school curriculum that presents Okanagan history in an accurate and dignified way. Armstrong and her fellow members on the Okanagan Tribal Education Committee believe that Okanagan people must tell their own stories; therefore, the curriculum project created the Learning Institute, which provides adult Native people with skills in research and writing so that First Nations individuals can develop quality, correct, and appropriate information for the project.

Theytus Books Ltd., the first publishing house in Canada owned and operated by First Nations people, was established in 1980 as part of the curriculum project and continues to run as a division of the En'owkin Centre. The En'owkin Centre's programs help to provide Theytus with proficient employees who work collectively in efforts to produce and promote appropriate reading material and information created by Native authors, illustrators, and artists.

Armstrong was appointed as the Executive Director of the En'owkin Centre in 1986 and she carries on in this role to present day.

In 1989 Armstrong helped to establish the En'owkin School of International Writing and became its director as well as an instructor. The En'owkin School of International Writing is the first credit-giving creative writing school in Canada operated entirely by and for Aboriginal people.

Armstrong as Author

Armstrong's literary production increased in breadth and magnitude shortly after her 1978 graduation. She published two children's books in the early 1980s, *Enwhisteetkwa* (or *Walk in Water*) in 1982 and *Neekna and Chemai* the following year, and performed two years of research in preparation for writing *Slash*, her first and most famous novel.

Like the En'owkin Learning Centre, Theytus Books, and the En'owkin School of International Writing, Armstrong's novel *Slash*, which was published in 1985 by Theytus, originates from the Okanagan Indian Curriculum Project. Commissioned for use as part of a grade eleven study in contemporary history, Armstrong wanted *Slash* to connect with and relate to contemporary students. Furthermore, Armstrong assumed the project in order to anticipate the work of more famous non-Aboriginal authors who were "dripping at the mouth" to document Native history.

Slash relates a history of the North American Indian protest movement through the critical perspective of central character Tommy Kelasket, who is eventually renamed Slash. Despite the intolerance that Tommy encounters in an assimilationist school system and racist North American society, his family encourages him to be proud of his Okanagan heritage and he eventually becomes an activist for Aboriginal rights. Armstrong clearly states that *Slash* is not a chronicle of AIM (American Indian Movement) from the AIM point of view; rather, the text provides a personalized account of the origins and growth of Native activism since the 1960s.

Since the appearance of *Slash* on the Canadian literary scene, Jeannette Armstrong has continued to write and publish widely. Armstrong s poetry appears in anthologies and her collection *Breath Tracks* (1991). Her short stories are collected in works such as *All My Relations: An Anthology of Contemporary Canadian Native Fiction* edited by Thomas King. Armstrong's second novel, *Whispering in Shadows,* which traces the life experiences of a young Okanagan activist woman, was published in 2000.

In addition to her creative works, Armstrong has published and continues to compose a wealth of critical works such as *The Native Creative Process,* a collaborative discourse between Armstrong and Douglas Cardinal on Aboriginal artistry, and "Land Speaking," which addresses how land and Okanagan language influence her writing.

Armstrong as Activist

In addition to the activism, Armstrong displays in her educational work, writing, and art, she is also a sought after speaker who serves on a number of committees that reflect her beliefs and interests.

She is a consultant to the Center for Ecoliteracy in Berkeley, California. This foundation encourages education that develops sustainable patterns of living. Moreover, she has acted as a consultant to social and environmental organizations such as the Centre for Creative Change, Esalen Institute, Omega Institute, and the World Institute for Humanities at Salado ("Awardee").

As a campaigner for Aboriginal rights, Armstrong serves as an international observer to the Continental Coordinating Commission of Indigenous Peoples and Organizations. She was also named as one of seven Indigenous Judges to the First Nations Court of Justice called by the Chiefs of Ontario and to the Council of Listeners in the International Testimonials on Violations of Indigenous Sovereignty for the United Nations ("Awardee").

Criticism and Influence

In her study of Native literature, Penny Petrone includes Jeannette Armstrong amongst a young generation of university trained Aboriginal authors who contributed purposeful, exciting, and original creative works to Canadian literature during the 1980s.

Despite Armstrong's involvement in the 1980s upsurge of Aboriginal literary activity and her prolific work, in-depth scholarship on her writing principally examines her poetry and, more extensively, her first novel. Petrone, nevertheless, comments on Armstrong's poetry, describing it as "direct, unequivocal, and assertive, even aggressive".

The scholarship on *Slash*, however, is more abundant and varied. In a 1989 interview with Hartmut Lutz, Armstrong relates that some feminist scholars question her decision to select a male central character for her novel; however, Armstrong compellingly contends that female strength and male development are portrayed effectively through the perspective of Slash.

In the same interview, Armstrong notes, "I've been criticized by non-Native critics in terms of character development". She explains that she could not isolate the character of Slash from his community in order depict his individual nature and still compose the story for her people. Significantly, and consistent with the view she expresses in "Land Speaking,"

Armstrong argues that Slash's personal growth can be perceived through his relationships with his family and community.

In her study of *Slash*, Manina Jones catalogues a number of critical responses to the work and states that many academic articles concerning it relate the difficulties that audiences experience in their attempts to address Armstrong's novel. Jones also describes *Slash* as a work that refuses priority to speech or writing, insisting instead on a hybrid status.

As Jones and the critics to whom she refers demonstrate, *Slash* is unique in its aesthetic practice and didactic purpose. In *Slash*, therefore, Armstrong compels audiences to read and consider her text in ways that may be unfamiliar to them. Ultimately, an innovative critical reading approach is essential for the appreciation of her work and to achieve the aims of the Okanagan Indian Curriculum Project.

Armstrong is dedicated to the advancement of literature and the arts among First Nations people and the realization and promotion of the distinct artistic forms of Aboriginal people in the international arts and literary community. Armstrong's insights as an educator, creative force, and activist are respected by First Nations individuals and international audiences alike.

14

Literary Life of Mordecai Richler

Mordecai Richler, CC (January 27, 1931 – July 3, 2001) was a Canadian author, Academy Award-nominated screenwriter and essayist. A leading critic called him "the great shining star of his Canadian literary generation" and a pivotal figure in the country's history. His best known works are *The Apprenticeship of Duddy Kravitz, Barney's Version,* and the *Jacob Two-Two* children's stories. Richler's uncompromising opinions on contemporary Canada easily matched, and sometimes exceeded, the satirical sting of his fiction.

Early Years

The son of a scrapyard dealer, Richler was born and raised on St. Urbain Street in the Mile End area of Montreal, Quebec, a neighbourhood he would later immortalize in his novels. He graduated from Baron Byng High School. Richler then enrolled in Sir George Williams College (now Concordia University) to study English but dropped out before completing his degree. He moved to Paris, France at age nineteen, intent on following in the footsteps of a previous generation of literary exiles, the so-called Lost Generation of the 1920s. Richler returned to Montreal in 1952, working briefly at the Canadian Broadcasting Corporation, then moved to London, England in 1954. Worrying "about being so long away from the roots of my discontent", he returned to Montreal in 1972, but continued to spend part of each year in London.

The Apprenticeship of Duddy Kravitz

Richler's career took off with the publication of his fourth novel *The Apprenticeship of Duddy Kravitz* in 1959. The book featured a frequent Richler theme: Jewish life in the 1930s and 40s in the neighbourhood of Montreal east of Mount Royal Park on and about St. Urbain Street and the Main (Boul. St. Laurent). Richler wrote poignantly of the neighbourhood and its people, chronicling the hardships and disabilities they faced as a Jewish minority.

To a middle-class stranger, it is true, one street would have seemed as squalid as the next. On each corner a cigar store, a grocery, and a fruit man. Outside staircases everywhere. Winding ones, wooden ones, rusty and risky ones. Here a prized lot of grass splendidly barbered, there a spitefully weedy patch. An endless repetition of precious peeling balconies and waste lots making the occasional gap here and there.

The 1974 movie version was directed by Richler's friend Ted Kotcheff and starred Richard Dreyfuss in his first leading role. Richler and Lionel Chetwynd co-wrote the screenplay.

Richler as Commentator

Throughout his career, Richler wrote acerbic journalistic commentary and delighted in the role of contrarian provocateur. He was an iconoclast with little tolerance for pretense or pomposity. In a characteristic putdown, Richler called Canadian film entrepreneurs "snivelling little greasers on the make." Richler contributed to *The Atlantic Monthly, Look,* and *The New Yorker*. In his later years, Richler was a newspaper columnist for *The National Post* and Montreal's *The Gazette*. He was often critical of Quebec and Canadian nationalism. Another favorite Richler target was the government-subsidized Canadian literary movement of the 1970s and 80s. Richler was made a Companion of the Order of Canada in 2001, just a few months before his death.

Proponents and Critics

Many critics distinguished between Richler the author and Richler the polemicist. Richler frequently said in interviews that his goal was to be an honest witness to his time and place, and to write at least one book that would be read after his death. His work was championed by journalists Robert Fulford and Peter Gzowski, among others. Admirers praised Richler for daring to tell uncomfortable truths, and he has been described in The Oxford Companion to Canadian Literature as "one of the foremost writers of his generation". A 2004 oral biography by Michael Posner was entitled *The Last Honest Man.*

Detractors called Richler's satire heavy-handed and noted his propensity for recycling material, incorporating elements of his journalism into later novels. Some critics thought Richler more adept at sketching striking scenes than crafting coherent narratives. Richler's ambivalent relationship with Montreal's Jewish community was captured in *Mordecai and Me,* a book by Joel Yanofsky published in

2003. Richler's most frequent conflicts were with the Jewish community, English Canadian nationalists, and Quebec nationalists.

Richler's long-running dispute with Quebec nationalists was fuelled by magazine articles he wrote in American publications between the late 1970s and mid 1990s. The articles criticized Quebec's language laws, and separatism. Critics took particular exception to Richler's allegations of anti-semitism.

In *The Atlantic Monthly,* around the time of the first election of the Parti Québécois (PQ) in 1976, Richler linked the PQ to Nazism, by asserting that the theme song of the 1976 PQ campaign "À partir d'aujourd'hui, demain nous appartient" was a Nazi song, "Tomorrow belongs to me..." the chilling Hitler Youth song from *Cabaret.* Neither the remainder of the text, nor the music, are related.

Furthermore, the *Cabaret* song, never sung in Nazi Germany, was written in the 1960s by John Kander, a Jewish American lyricist and composer, not German fascists. "À partir d'aujourd'hui" was written by well-known songwriter Stéphane Venne when he was asked to compose a song for an advertisement of the Caisses populaires Desjardins credit union. In *Oh Canada! Oh Quebec!,* Richler acknowledges the error, blaming himself for having "cribbed" the information from an article by Irwin Cotler and Ruth Wisse for the Jewish American magazine *Commentary.* Co-writer of the *Commentary* article Cotler eventually issued a written apology to Lévesque. Richler also apologized for the incident and called it an "embarrassing gaffe".

His views were strongly criticized by some in Quebec and to some degree among Anglophone Canadians. His detractors maintained that Richler had an outdated and stereotyped view of Quebec society, and that he risked polarizing relations between French and English. After the publication of *Oh Canada! Oh Quebec,* Pierrette Venne, a future Bloc Québécois MP called for the book to be banned. Daniel Latouche compared the book to *Mein Kampf*. Nadia Khouri believes that there was a racist undertone in some of the reaction to Richler, emphasizing that he was not "one of us" or that he was not a "real Quebecer" Additionally some passages were deliberately misquoted; a section in which he said that Quebec women were treated like "sows" was misinterpreted to suggest that Richler thought they were sows. Other French writers also thought there had been an overreaction, including Jean-Hugues Roy, Étienne Gignac, Serge-Henri Vicière, and Dorval Brunelle. His defenders asserted that Mordecai Richler may have been wrong on certain specific points, but was certainly not racist or anti-Québécois. Richler had always attacked nationalists, including English Canadians, Israelis and Zionists. Some Quebecers acclaimed Richler for his courage and for attacking the orthodoxies of Quebec society, and he has been described as "the most prominent defender of the rights of Quebec's anglophones."

The reaction to Richler's book itself raised concerns for some commentators about the persistence of antisemitism among sections of the Quebec population. He received death threats, including a threat to blow up the hospital in which he was staying, and letters with swastikas drawn on them; a Francophone journalist yelled at one of his sons that "if your father was here, I'd make him relive the holocaust right now!", while an editorial cartoon in the French press compared him to Hitler. The criticism that he wrote his essay on Quebec for money was seen as evoking old stereotypes of Jews, and the demands made for leaders of the Jewish community to dissociate themselves from Richler were seen as indicating that Richler, although born in Quebec and for a time married to a French-Canadian, was "not part of the tribe" because he was anglo and Jewish.

Following Jacques Parizeau's comment on the day of the 1995 referendum, where the latter attributed the loss to "money and the ethnic vote", Richler created the "Impure Wool Society" which granted the *"Prix Parizeau"* to a distinguished non-Francophone writer of Quebec. The group's name plays on the expression "québécois pure laine", typically used to refer to Québécois with extensive French-Canadian ancestry. The prize (with an award of $3000) was granted twice: Benet Davetian in 1996 for *The Seventh Circle,* and David Manicom in 1997 for *Ice In Dark Water.*

Animator Caroline Leaf created an Academy Award-nominated animation in 1976 titled *The Street,* based on Richler's 1969 short story of the same name.

Family Life

Richler divorced Catherine Boudreault to marry his second wife, Florence. He adopted her son Daniel. The couple had five children, including:

1. Daniel Richler - A longstanding figure in Canadian media and broadcasting, Daniel Richler has written a semi-autobiographical novel, *Kicking Tomorrow* (1991). The protagonist's father bears many similarities to Mordecai Richler.
2. Emma Richler - author of a collection of linked short stories *Sister Crazy* (2001), which features a

father modeled on her own. A novel, *Feed My Dear Dogs* was published in 2005.

3. Jacob Richler - an author and columnist.
4. Noah Richler - a journalist, radio producer and host, and author of *This Is My Country, What's Yours? A Literary Atlas of Canada* (2006).
5. Martha Richler - a cartoonist who published a daily cartoon, most recently, in London's *Evening Standard*, using the pen-name "Marf". Her cartoons are in the collection of the Victoria & Albert Museum, London, and the Charles Saatchi Collection. She also wrote the companion guide to Washington's National Gallery of Art, *A World of Art*.

Leah Rosenberg, Richler's mother, published an autobiography, *The Errand Runner: Memoirs of a Rabbi's Daughter* (1981), which discusses Mordecai's birth and upbringing.

15

Literary Life of Stephen Leacock

Stephen Butler Leacock, FRSC (30 December 1869 – 28 March 1944) was a Canadian writer and economist.

Early Life

Leacock was born in Swanmore, near Bishop's Waltham, Hampshire, England, and at the age of six moved to Canada with his family, which settled on a farm in Egypt, Ontario, near the village of Sutton and the shores of Lake Simcoe. While the family had been well off in England (the Leacocks had made a fortune in Madeira and lived on an estate called Oak Hill on the Isle of Wight), Leacock's father, Peter, had been banished from the manor for marrying Agnes Butler without his parents' permission. The farm in the Georgina township of York County was not a success and the family (Leacock was the third of eleven children) was kept afloat by money sent by Leacock's grandfather. Peter Leacock became an alcoholic.

Leacock, always of obvious intelligence, was sent by his grandfather to the elite private school of Upper Canada College in Toronto, also attended by his older brothers, where he was top of the class and was chosen as head boy. In 1887, defending his mother and siblings against his father's alcoholic abuse, Leacock ordered him from the family home and he was never seen again. That same year, seventeen-year-old Leacock started at University College at the University of Toronto, where he was admitted to the Zeta Psi fraternity, but found he could not resume the following year as a consequence of financial difficulties.

He left university to go to work teaching — an occupation he disliked immensely — at Strathroy, Uxbridge and finally in Toronto. As a teacher at Upper Canada College, his *alma mater*, he was able to simultaneously attend classes at the University of Toronto and, in 1891, earn his degree through part-time studies. It was during this period that his first writing was published in *The Varsity*, a campus newspaper.

Academic and Political Life

Disillusioned with teaching, in 1899 he began graduate studies at the University of Chicago where he received a doctorate in political science and political economy. He moved from Chicago, Illinois to Montreal, Quebec where he became a lecturer and long-time acting head of the political economy department at McGill University.

He was closely associated with Sir Arthur Currie, former commander of the Canadian Corps in the Great War and principal of McGill from 1919 until his death in 1933. In fact, Currie had been a student observing Leacock's practice teaching in Strathroy in 1888. In 1936, Leacock was forcibly retired by the McGill Board of Governors — an unlikely prospect had Currie lived.

Leacock was both a social conservative and a partisan Conservative. He opposed women's rights (including the right to vote), and disliked non-Anglo-Saxon immigration. He was, however, a supporter of social welfare legislation. He was a staunch champion of the British Empire, and went on lecture tours to further the cause.

Although he was considered as a Federal candidate for his party, it declined to invite the author, lecturer and maverick to stand for election. Nevertheless, he would stump for local candidates at his summer home.

Literary Life

Early in his career, Leacock turned to fiction, humour, and short reports to supplement (and ultimately exceed) his regular income. His stories, first published in magazines in Canada and the United States and later in novel form, became extremely popular around the world. It was said in 1911 that more people had heard of Stephen Leacock than had heard of Canada. Also, between the years 1915 and 1925, Leacock was the most popular humourist in the English-speaking world.

Humorists admire other humorists, and greatly admire other great humorists. So it was that Stephen Leacock, in Toronto, was delighted to read the fresh humor and wit of a young man in New York named Robert Benchley. Leacock opened correspondence with Benchley, encouraging him in his work and importuning him to compile his work into a book. Benchly did so in 1922, and acknowledged the nagging from north of the border.

Near the end of his life, the American comedian Jack Benny recounted how he had been introduced to Leacock's writing by Groucho Marx when they were both young vaudeville comedians. Benny acknowledged Leacock's influence and, fifty years after first reading him, still considered Leacock one of his favorite comic writers. He was puzzled as to why Leacock's work was no longer well-known in the United States.

During the summer months, Leacock lived at Old Brewery Bay, his summer estate in Orillia, across Lake Simcoe from where he was raised and also bordering Lake Couchiching. A working farm, Old Brewery Bay is now a museum and National Historic Site. Gossip provided by the local barber, Jefferson Short, provided Leacock with the material which would become *Sunshine Sketches of a Little Town* (1912), set in the thinly-disguised Mariposa.

Although he wrote learned articles and books related to his field of study, his political theory is now all but forgotten. Leacock was awarded the Royal Society of Canada's Lorne Pierce Medal in 1937, nominally for his academic work.

Death and Tributes

In 1900 Leacock married Beatrix ("Trix") Hamilton, niece of Sir Henry Pellatt (who had built Casa Loma, the largest castle in North America). In 1915 – after 15 years of marriage – the couple had their only child, Stephen Lushington Leacock. While Leacock doted on the boy, it became apparent early on that "Stevie" suffered from a lack of growth hormone. Growing to be only four feet tall, he had a love-hate relationship with Leacock, who tended to treat him like a child.

Predeceased by Trix (who had died of breast cancer in 1925), Leacock was survived by Stevie, who died in his fifties. In accordance with his wishes, after his death from throat cancer, Leacock was cremated and buried at Sibbald Point in Georgina Township, near his boyhood home and across Lake Simcoe from his summer home.

Shortly after his death, Barbara Nimmo, his niece, literary executor and benefactor, published two major posthumous works: *Last Leaves* (1945) and *The Boy I Left Behind Me* (1946). His physical legacy was less treasured, and his abandoned summer cottage became derelict. It was rescued from oblivion when it was declared a National Historic Site in 1958 and ever since has operated as a museum called the Stephen Leacock Memorial Home.

In 1947, the Stephen Leacock Award was created to recognize the best in Canadian literary humour. In 1969, the centennial of his birth, Canada Post issued a six cent stamp with his image on it. The following year, the Stephen Leacock Centennial Committee had a plaque erected at his English birthplace and a mountain in the Yukon was named after him.

A number of buildings in Canada are named after Leacock, including the Stephen Leacock Building at McGill University, a theatre in Keswick, Ontario, and schools in Toronto and Ottawa.

16

Literary Life of Alice Munro

Alice Ann Munro (née Laidlaw; born 10 July 1931) is a Canadian short-story writer, winner of the 2009 Man Booker International Prize for her lifetime body of work, and three-time winner of Canada's Governor General's Award for fiction. Generally regarded to be one of the world's foremost writers of fiction, her stories focus on the human condition and relationships through the lens of daily life. While the locus of Munro's fiction is Southwestern Ontario, her reputation as a short-story writer is international. Her "accessible, moving stories" explore human complexities in a seemingly effortless style. Munro's writing has established her as "one of our greatest contemporary writers of fiction," or, as Cynthia Ozick put it, "our Chekhov."

Life and Career

Munro was born in the town of Wingham, Ontario into a family of fox and poultry farmers. Her father was Robert Eric Laidlaw and her mother, a school teacher, was Anne Clarke Laidlaw (née Chamney). She began writing as a teenager and published her first story, "The Dimensions of a Shadow," while a student at the

University of Western Ontario in 1950. During this period she worked as a waitress, tobacco picker and library clerk. In 1951, she left the university, in which she had been majoring in English since 1949, to marry James Munro and move to Vancouver, British Columbia. Her daughters Sheila, Catherine, and Jenny were born in 1953, 1955, and 1957 respectively; Catherine died 15 hours after birth. In 1963, the Munros moved to Victoria where they opened Munro's Books. In 1966, their daughter Andrea was born.

Alice Munro's first collection of stories, *Dance of the Happy Shades* (1968), was highly acclaimed and won that year's Governor General's Award, Canada's highest literary prize. This success was followed by *Lives of Girls and Women* (1971), a collection of interlinked stories that was published as a novel.

Alice and James Munro were divorced in 1972. She returned to Ontario to become Writer-in-Residence at the University of Western Ontario. In 1976 she married Gerald Fremlin, a geographer. The couple moved to a farm outside Clinton, Ontario. They have since moved from the farm to a house in the town of Clinton.

In 1978, Munro's collection of interlinked stories, *Who Do You Think You Are?*, was published (titled *The Beggar Maid: Stories of Flo and Rose* in the United States). This book earned Munro the Governor General's Literary Award for a second time. From 1979 to 1982, she toured Australia, China and Scandinavia. In 1980 Munro held the position of Writer-in-Residence at both the University of British Columbia and the University of Queensland. Through the 1980s and 1990s, Munro published a short-story collection about once every four years to increasing acclaim, winning both national and international awards.

In 2002, her daughter Sheila Munro published a childhood memoir, *Lives of Mothers and Daughters: Growing Up With Alice Munro.*

Alice Munro's stories frequently appear in publications such as *The New Yorker, The Atlantic Monthly, Grand Street, Mademoiselle,* and *The Paris Review.* In interviews to promote her 2006 collection *The View from Castle Rock,* Munro suggested that she would, perhaps, not publish any further collections. She has since recanted and published further work. Her latest collection, *Too Much Happiness,* was published in August 2009.

Her story "The Bear Came Over the Mountain" has been adapted for the screen and directed by Sarah Polley as the film *Away from Her,* starring Julie Christie and Gordon Pinsent. It successfully debuted at the 2006 Toronto International Film Festival. Polley's adaptation was nominated for an Academy Award for Best Adapted Screenplay, but lost to *No Country for Old Men.*

Writing Style

Many of Munro's stories are set in Huron County, Ontario. Her strong regional focus is one of the features of her fiction. Another is the all-knowing narrator who serves to make sense of the world. Many compare Munro's small-town settings to writers of the U.S. rural South. As in the works of William Faulkner and Flannery O'Connor, her characters often confront deep-rooted customs and traditions. However, the reaction of Munro's characters is less intense than their Southern counterparts'. Thus, particularly with respect to her male characters, she may be said to **capture** the essence of everyman. Her female characters, though, are more complex. Much of Munro's work exemplifies the literary genre known as Southern Ontario Gothic.

Munro's work is often compared with the great short story writers. For example, the American writer Cynthia Ozick called Munro "our Chekhov." In Munro stories, as in Chekhov's, plot is secondary and "little happens." As with Chekhov, Garan Holcombe notes: "All is based on the epiphanic moment, the sudden enlightenment, the concise, subtle, revelatory detail." Munro's work deals with "love and work, and the failings of both. She shares Chekhov's obsession with time and our much-lamented inability to delay or prevent its relentless movement forward."

A frequent theme of her work--particularly evident in her early stories—has been the dilemmas of a girl coming of age and coming to terms with her family and the small town she grew up in. In recent work such as *Hateship, Friendship, Courtship, Loveship, Marriage* (2001) and *Runaway* (2004) she has shifted her focus to the travails of middle age, of women alone and of the elderly. It is a mark of her style for characters to experience a revelation that sheds light on, and gives meaning to, an event.

Munro's spare and lucid language and command of detail gives her fiction a "remarkable precision," as Helen Hoy observes. Munro's prose reveals the ambiguities of life: "ironic and serious at the same time," "mottoes of godliness and honor and flaming bigotry," "special, useless knowledge," "tones of shrill and happy outrage," "the bad taste, the heartlessness, the joy of it." Her style places the fantastic next to the ordinary with each undercutting the other in ways that simply, and effortlessly, evoke life. As Robert Thacker notes:

> Munro's writing creates... an empathetic union among readers, critics most apparent among them. We are drawn to her writing by its verisimilitude—not of mimesis, so-called and... 'realism'—but rather the feeling of being itself... of just being a human being.

Many critics have asserted that Munro's stories often have the emotional and literary depth of novels. The question of whether Munro actually writes short-stories or novels has often been asked. Alex Keegan, writing in *Eclectica,* has a simple answer: "Who cares? In most Munro stories there is as much as in many novels."

17

Writings of Leonard Cohen

Leonard Norman Cohen, (born September 21, 1934) is a Canadian singer-songwriter, musician, poet and novelist. Cohen published his first book of poetry in Montreal in 1956 and his first novel in 1963. His work often deals with the exploration of religion, isolation, sexuality and complex interpersonal relationships. Famously reclusive, spending years in a Zen Buddhist monastery, and possessing a persona frequently associated with mystique, he is extremely well-regarded by critics for his literary accomplishments and for producing an output of work of high artistic quality over a five-decade career.

Musically, Cohen's earliest songs (many of which appeared on the 1967 album, *Songs of Leonard Cohen*) were rooted in European folk music. In the 1970s, his material encompassed pop, cabaret and world music. Since the 1980s his high baritone voice has evolved into lower registers (bass baritone and bass), with accompaniment from a wide variety of instruments and female backing singers.

Over 2,000 renditions of Cohen's songs have been recorded. Cohen has been inducted into both the Canadian Music Hall of Fame and the Canadian

Songwriters Hall of Fame and is also a Companion of the Order of Canada, the nation's highest civilian honour. While giving the speech at Cohen's induction into the American Rock and Roll Hall of Fame on March 10, 2008, Lou Reed described Cohen as belonging to the "highest and most influential echelon of songwriters".

Early Life

Cohen was born in 1934 in Westmount, Montreal, Quebec, into a middle-class Jewish family. His mother, of Lithuanian Jewish ancestry, emigrated from Lithuania while his great-grandfather emigrated from Poland. He grew up in Westmount on the Island of Montreal. His father, Nathan Cohen, owned a substantial Montreal clothing store, and died when Leonard was nine years old. Like many other Jewish families with names like Cohen, Kahn, and Kagan, Cohen's family claimed descent from the Kohanim: "I had a very Messianic childhood", he told Richard Goldstein in 1967. "I was told I was a descendant of Aaron, the high priest." He attended Herzliah High School, where he studied with poet Irving Layton. As a teenager he learned to play the guitar, subsequently forming a country-folk group called the Buckskin Boys. His father's will provided Leonard with a modest trust income, sufficient to allow him to pursue his literary ambitions.

Poetry

In 1951, Cohen enrolled at McGill University, where he became president of the McGill Debating Union. His literary influences during this time included Yeats, Irving Layton, Whitman, Federico Garcia Lorca and

Henry Miller. His first published book of poetry, *Let Us Compare Mythologies* (1956), was published under Louis Dudek as the first book in the McGill Poetry Series while Cohen was still an undergraduate student. *The Spice-Box of Earth* (1961) made him well known in poetry circles, especially in his native Canada.

After completing an undergraduate degree, Cohen spent a term in McGill's law school and a year (1956-7) at Columbia University.

Cohen applied a strong work ethic to his early and keen literary ambitions. He wrote poetry and fiction through much of the 1960s, and preferred to live in quasi-reclusive circumstances. After moving to Hydra, a Greek island, Cohen published the poetry collection *Flowers for Hitler* (1964), and the novels *The Favourite Game* (1963) and *Beautiful Losers* (1966). *The Favourite Game* is an autobiographical *bildungsroman* about a young man who discovers his identity through writing.

Cohen's writing process, he told an interviewer in 1998, is "like a bear stumbling into a beehive or a honey cache: I'm stumbling right into it and getting stuck, and it's delicious and it's horrible and I'm in it and it's not very graceful and it's very awkward and it's very painful and yet there's something inevitable about it."

Recording Career

1960s and 1970s

In 1967, Cohen moved to the United States to pursue a career as a folk music singer-songwriter. During the 60s, he was a fringe figure in Andy Warhol's Factory crowd. Warhol speculated that Cohen had spent time listening to Nico in clubs and that this had influenced his musical style. His song "Suzanne" became a hit for Judy Collins and was for many years his most covered song. After performing at a few folk festivals, he came to the attention of Columbia Records representative John H. Hammond.

Cohen's first album, *Songs of Leonard Cohen* (1967), was too dark to be a commercial success but was widely acclaimed by folk music buffs. He became a cult name in the UK, where the album spent over a year on the album charts. He followed it with *Songs from a Room* (1969) (featuring the often recorded "Bird on the Wire"), *Songs of Love and Hate* (1971), *Live Songs* (1973) and *New Skin for the Old Ceremony* (1974).

In 1971, Cohen's music was used in the soundtrack to Robert Altman's film *McCabe & Mrs. Miller*. Cohen had been in Nashville when Altman phoned to ask permission to use some tracks off *Songs of Leonard Cohen*. Coincidentally, earlier that same day, Cohen had viewed Altman's film, *Brewster McCloud*, in a Nashville theater. He hadn't paid attention to the credits, though; when Altman asked permission to use Cohen's songs in his new film, Cohen asked him who, exactly, he was. Altman mentioned *MASH*, but Cohen had never heard of it. Altman then told him of the lesser-known *Brewster McCloud*. Cohen, likely astonished, replied, "Listen, I just came out of the theater. I saw it twice; you can have anything of mine you want!"

In the late 1960s and early 1970s, Cohen toured the United States, Canada and Europe. Beginning around 1974, his collaboration with pianist and arranger John Lissauer created a live sound praised by the critics. During this time, Cohen toured twice with

Jennifer Warnes as a back-up singer (in 1972 and 1979). Warnes would become a fixture on Cohen's future albums and she recorded an album of Cohen songs in 1987, *Famous Blue Raincoat.*

In 1977, Cohen released *Death of a Ladies' Man* (note the plural possessive case; one year later in 1978, Cohen released a volume of poetry with the coyly revised title, *Death of a Lady's Man*). The album was produced by Phil Spector, well known as the inventor of the "wall of sound" technique, in which pop music is backed with thick layers of instrumentation, an approach very different from Cohen's usually minimalist instrumentation. The recording of the album was fraught with difficulty; Spector reportedly mixed the album in secret studio sessions, and Cohen said Spector once threatened him with a crossbow. Cohen thought the end result to be "grotesque", but also "semi-virtuous".

In 1979, Cohen returned with the more traditional *Recent Songs.* Produced by Cohen himself and Henry Lewy (Joni Mitchell's sound engineer) the album included performances by a jazz-fusion band introduced to Cohen by Mitchell and oriental instruments (oud, Gypsy violin and mandolin). In 2001 Cohen released an album of live recordings of songs from his 1979 tour, entitled *Field Commander Cohen: Tour of 1979.*

1980s

In 1984, Cohen released *Various Positions,* including "Dance Me to the End of Love" and the often recorded "Hallelujah". Columbia declined to release the album in the United States, where Cohen's popularity had declined in previous years. Throughout his career,

Cohen's music has sold better in Europe and Canada than in the U.S.; he once satirically expressed how touched he is at the modesty the American company showed in promoting his records.

In 1986 he appeared in the episode *French Twist* of the TV series *Miami Vice.* In 1987, Jennifer Warnes's tribute album *Famous Blue Raincoat* helped restore Cohen's career in the U.S., and the following year he released *I'm Your Man,* which marked a drastic change in his music. Synthesizers ruled the album and Cohen's lyrics included more social commentary and dark humour. It was Cohen's most acclaimed and popular since *Songs of Leonard Cohen.* "First We Take Manhattan" and the title song became two of his most popular songs.

1990s

The use of the album track "Everybody Knows" (co-written by Sharon Robinson) in the 1990 film *Pump Up the Volume* helped to expose Cohen's music to a younger audience. The song was also featured prominently in fellow countryman Atom Egoyan's 1994 film, *Exotica.* In 1992, Cohen released *The Future,* which urges (often in terms of biblical prophecy) perseverance, reformation, and hope in the face of grim prospects. Three tracks from the album - "Waiting for the Miracle", "The Future" and "Anthem" - were featured in the movie *Natural Born Killers.*

In the title track, Cohen prophesies impending political and social collapse, reportedly as his response to the L.A. unrest of 1992: "I've seen the future, brother: It is murder." In "Democracy", Cohen criticizes America but says he loves it: "I love the country but I can't stand the scene." Further, he criticizes the American public's lack of interest in politics and addiction to television: "I'm neither left or right/I'm just staying home tonight/getting lost in that hopeless little screen".

Nanni Moretti's film *Caro diario* (1993) features "I'm Your Man", as Moretti himself rides his Vespa along the streets of Rome.

In 1994, following a tour to promote *The Future,* Cohen retreated to the Mt. Baldy Zen Center near Los Angeles, beginning what would become five years of seclusion at the center. In 1996, Cohen was ordained as a Rinzai Zen Buddhist monk and took the Dharma name *Jikan,* meaning 'silence'. He served as personal assistant to Kyozan Joshu Sasaki Roshi. He left Mount Baldy in 1999. Japanese songwriter and poet Masato Tomobe stated he admires Cohen and made him more recognized in Japan around this time.

2000s

Ten New Songs

In 2001, following the five years' seclusion as a Zen Buddhist monk at the Mt. Baldy Zen Center, Cohen returned to music with *Ten New Songs,* featuring a heavy influence from producer and co-composer Sharon Robinson. With this album, Cohen shed the relatively extroverted, engaged, and even optimistic outlook of *The Future* (the sole political track, "The Land of Plenty," abandoning stern commandment for yearning but helpless prayer) to lament and seek acceptance of varieties of personal loss: the approach of death and the departure of love, romantic and even divine. *Ten New Songs'* cohesive musical style (perhaps absent from Cohen's albums since *Recent Songs*) owes much to Robinson's involvement. The album includes the song "Alexandra Leaving", which is a striking transformation of the poem "The God Abandons Antony", by the Greek poet Constantine P. Cavafy. Although not Cohen's bitterest album, it may rank as his most melancholic.

Dear Heather

In October 2004, Cohen released *Dear Heather,* largely a musical collaboration with jazz chanteuse (and current romantic partner) Anjani Thomas, although Sharon Robinson returns to collaborate on three tracks (including a duet). As light as the previous album was dark, *Dear Heather* reflects Cohen's own change of mood - he has said in a number of interviews that his depression has lifted in recent years, which he attributes to the aid of Zen Buddhism. *Dear Heather* is perhaps his least cohesive, and most experimental and playful album to date, and the stylings of some of the songs (especially the title track) frustrated many fans. In an interview following his induction into the Canadian Songwriters' Hall of Fame, Cohen explained that the album was intended to be a kind of notebook or scrapbook of themes, and that a more formal record had been planned for release shortly afterwards, but that this was put on ice by his legal battles with his ex-manager.

Blue Alert

Blue Alert, an album of songs co-written by Anjani and Cohen, was released on May 23, 2006 to positive reviews. The album is sung by Anjani, who according to one reviewer "sounds like Cohen reincarnated as woman.... though Cohen doesn't sing a note on the album, his voice permeates it like smoke." The album includes a recent musical setting of Cohen's "As the mist leaves no scar", a poem originally published in *The Spice-Box of Earth* in 1961 and adapted by Spector into "True Love Leaves No Traces" on *Death of a Ladies' Man.*

Book of Longing

Cohen's book of poetry and drawings, *Book of Longing,* was published in May 2006; in March a Toronto-based retailer offered signed copies to the first 1500 orders placed online, which saw the entire amount sold within hours. The book quickly topped bestseller lists in Canada. On May 13, 2006, Cohen made his first public appearance for thirteen years, at an in-store event at a bookstore in Toronto. Approximately 3000 people turned up for the event, causing the streets surrounding the bookstore to be closed. He sang two of his earliest and best-known songs: "So Long, Marianne" and "Hey, That's No Way To Say Goodbye", accompanied by the Barenaked Ladies and Ron Sexsmith. Also appearing with him was Anjani, the two promoting her new CD, along with his book.

2008 Concert Tour

January 13, 2008, Cohen quietly announced a long-anticipated concert tour. The tour, Cohen's first in 15 years, began May 11 in Fredericton, NB to wide critical acclaim, and was prolonged until spring of 2010. The schedule encompassed Canada and Europe, including performances at The Big Chill (music festival), the Montreal Jazz Festival, and on the Pyramid Stage at the 2008 Glastonbury Festival on 29 June 2008. His performance at Glastonbury was hailed by many as the highlight of the festival, and his performance of 'Hallelujah' as the sun went down received a rapturous reception and a lengthy ovation from a packed Pyramid Stage field. He also played in Dublin in what has come to be regarded as a "milestone concert". The London performance was later released on CD and DVD under the title *Live in London.*

The Sydney Entertainment Centre show on January 28 sold out rapidly, which motivated promoters to later announce a second show at the venue. The first performance was well-received, and the audience of 12,000 responded with five standing ovations. Cohen gave generous credit to his touring band, his long-time collaborator and vocalist Sharon Robinson, and the "sublime" Webb Sisters. In January 2009, the tour arrived in New Zealand. Simon Sweetman in The Dominion Post (Wellington) of 21 January wrote "It is hard work having to put this concert in to words so I'll just say something I have never said in a review before and will never say again: this was the best show I have ever seen." The first concert of the Australian tour took place at Rochford Winery in Victoria's Yarra Valley on January 24 in perfect weather in front of an audience of about 7,000.

Hallelujah

On March 7, 2008, Jeff Buckley's version of Cohen's "Hallelujah", went to number 1 on the iTunes chart after being performed by Jason Castro on the seventh season of the television series *American Idol.* Another major boost for Cohen's song exposure came when singer-songwriter Kate Voegele released her version of "Hallelujah" from her 2007 *Don't Look Away* album and appeared as a regular character, named Mia, on season five of the teenage television show *One Tree Hill.*

A few days later, Cohen was inducted into the American Rock and Roll Hall of Fame in recognition of his status among the "highest and most influential echelon of songwriters".. He was introduced by fellow musician Lou Reed.

Live in London

On March 21, 2009, Cohen released "Live in London", which was recorded on July 17, 2008 at London's O2 Arena, and was released in both DVD and as a two-CD set. The album contains 27 songs and is over two and a half hours long.

2009 Concerts

On February 19, 2009, Cohen played his first American concert in fifteen years at the Beacon Theatre in New York City. He also performed at the Coachella Valley Music and Arts Festival on Friday, April 17, 2009, in front of one of the largest Outdoor Theatre crowds in the history of the festival. His performance of "Hallelujah" was widely regarded as one of the highlights of the festival.

In February 2009, in response to hearing about the devastation to the Yarra Valley region of Victoria in Australia, he donated $200,000 to the Victorian Bushfire Appeal in support of those affected by the extensive Black Saturday bushfires that razed the area just weeks after his performance at the Rochford Winery in the *A Day on the Green* concert. Melbourne's Herald Sun newspaper reported: "Tour promoter Frontier Touring said $200,000 would be donated on behalf of Cohen, [fellow performer Paul] Kelly and Frontier to aid victims of the Victorian bushfires."

A scheduled concert in Ramallah was cancelled after Palestinian human-rights activists objected to the fact that Cohen had also scheduled a concert in Tel Aviv, Israel, contrary to a proposed cultural boycott of Israel. Tickets for the Tel Aviv concert, Cohen's first performance in Israel since 1975, went on sale on August 1, 2009, and were sold out in less than 24 hours. It was announced that proceeds from the sale of the 47,000 tickets would go into a charitable fund in partnership with Amnesty International and would be used by Israeli and Palestinian peace groups for projects providing health services to children and bringing together Israeli veterans and former Palestinian fighters and the families of those killed in the conflict. However on August 17, 2009, Amnesty International released a statement saying they were withdrawing from any involvement with the concert or its proceeds. Amnesty International later stated that its withdrawal was not due to the boycott but "the lack of support from Israeli and Palestinian NGOs." The Palestinian Campaign for the Academic and Cultural Boycott of Israel (PACBI) led the call for the boycott, claiming that Cohen "is intent on whitewashing Israel's colonial apartheid regime by performing in Israel."

On September 18, at a concert in Valencia, Spain, Cohen collapsed halfway through performing his song *Bird on the Wire*. It was reported that Cohen had stomach problems, and possibly food poisoning.

On September 24 at the Ramat Gan Stadium, Israel, Cohen was highly emotional about the Israeli-Palestinian NGO Bereaved Families for Peace. He mentioned the organization twice, saying "It was a while ago that I first heard of the work of the

'Bereaved Parents for Peace'. That there was this coalition of Palestinian and Israeli families who had lost so much in the conflict and whose depth of suffering had compelled them to reach across the border into the houses of the enemy. Into the houses of those, to locate them who had suffered as much as they had, and then to stand with them in aching confraternity, a witness to an understanding that is beyond peace and that is beyond confrontation. So, this is not about forgiving and forgetting, this is not about laying down one's arms in a time of war, this is not even about peace, although, god willing, it could be a beginning. This is about a response to human grief. A radical, unique and holy, holy, holy response to human suffering. Baruch Hashem, thank God, I bow my head in respect to the nobility of this enterprise." At the end of the show he blessed the crowd by the Priestly Blessing, a Jewish blessing offered by Kohanim.

Themes

Recurring themes in Cohen's work include love and sex, religion, psychological depression, and music itself. He has also engaged with certain political themes, though sometimes ambiguously so. "Suzanne" mixes a wistful type of love song with a religious meditation, themes that are also mixed in "Joan of Arc". "Famous Blue Raincoat" is from the point of view of a man whose marriage has been broken (in exactly what degree is ambiguous in the song) by his wife's infidelity with his close friend, and is written in the form of a letter to that friend, to whom he writes, "I guess that I miss you/ I guess I forgive you ... Know your enemy is sleeping/ And his woman is free", while "Everybody Knows" deals in part with social inequality ("...the poor stay poor/ And the rich get rich"), and the harsh reality of AIDS: "... the naked man and woman/ Are just a shining artifact of the past".

"Sisters of Mercy", according to the sleeve notes of his *Greatest Hits* evokes his encounter with two women named Barbara and Lorraine in a hotel room in Edmonton, Canada. Claims that "Chelsea Hotel #2" treats his affair with Janis Joplin without sentimentality are countered by claims that the song reveals a much more complicated and mixed set of feelings than straightforward love. Cohen discusses the song in an interview filmed for the tribute-concert movie Leonard Cohen: I'm Your Man. He confirms that the subject is indeed Janis with some evident embarrassment. "She wouldn't mind", he declares, "but my mother would be appalled". The title of "Don't Go Home with Your Hard-On" speaks for itself.

Cohen comes from a Jewish background, most obviously reflected in his song "Story of Isaac", and also in "Who by Fire", whose words and melody echo the Unetaneh Tokef, an 11th century liturgical poem recited on Rosh Hashana and Yom Kippur. Broader Judeo-Christian themes are sounded throughout the album *Various Positions*: "Hallelujah", which has music as a secondary theme, begins by evoking the biblical king David composing a song that "pleased the Lord", and continues with references to Bathsheba and Samson. The lyrics of "Whither Thou Goest", performed by him and released in his album "Live in London", are adapted from the Bible (Ruth 1:16-17, King James Version). *If it be Your Will* also has a strong air of religious resignation.

In his concert in Ramat Gan, Israel, on the 24th of September 2009 Cohen spoke to the audience in Hebrew when using Jewish prayers and blessings. He opened the show with the first sentence of Ma Tovu. At the middle he used Baruch Hashem, and he ended the concert reciting the blessing of Birkat Cohanim.

In his early career as a novelist, *Beautiful Losers* grappled with the mysticism of the Catholic/Iroquois Catherine Tekakwitha. Cohen has also been involved with Buddhism at least since the 1970s and in 1996 he was ordained a Buddhist monk. However, he still considers himself also a Jew: "I'm not looking for a new religion. I'm quite happy with the old one, with Judaism."

He is described as an observant Jew in an article in *The New York Times*:

Mr. Cohen is an observant Jew who keeps the Sabbath even while on tour and performed for Israeli troops during the 1973 Arab-Israeli war. So how does he square that faith with his continued practice of Zen?

"Allen Ginsberg asked me the same question many years ago," he said. "Well, for one thing, in the tradition of Zen that I've practiced, there is no prayerful worship and there is no affirmation of a deity. So theologically there is no challenge to any Jewish belief."

Having suffered from depression during much of his life (although less so with the onset of old age), Cohen has written much (especially in his early work) about depression and suicide. The wife of the protagonist of *Beautiful Losers* commits a gory suicide; "Seems So Long Ago, Nancy" is about a suicide; suicide is mentioned in the darkly comic "One of Us

Cannot Be Wrong"; "Dress Rehearsal Rag" is about a last-minute decision not to kill oneself; a general atmosphere of depression pervades such songs as "Please Don't Pass Me By" and "Tonight Will Be Fine". As in the aforementioned "Hallelujah", music itself is the subject of many songs, including "Tower of Song", "A Singer Must Die", and "Jazz Police".

Social justice often shows up as a theme in his work, where he seems, especially in later albums, to expound a leftist politics, albeit with culturally conservative elements. In "Democracy", lamenting, "the wars against disorder/ ... the sirens night and day/ ... the fires of the homeless/ ... the ashes of the gay", he concludes that the United States is actually not a democracy. He has made the observation (in "Tower of Song") that, "the rich have got their channels in the bedrooms of the poor/ And there's a mighty judgment coming". In the title track of *The Future* he recasts this prophecy on a pacifist note: "I've seen the nations rise and fall/ .../ But love's the only engine of survival". In "Anthem", he promises that "the killers in high places [who] say their prayers out loud/ ... [are] gonna hear from me".

Several Cohen songs speak of abortion, always either as something distasteful or even atrocious. In "The Future", he sings sarcastically "Destroy another fetus now/ We don't like children anyhow". In "Stories of the Street" Cohen speaks of "The age of lust is giving birth/ And both the parents ask/ The nurse to tell them fairy tales/ from both sides of the glass".

"Diamonds in the Mine" is often quoted as being a song about abortion with the lyric: "The only man of energy/ Yes the revolution's pride/ He trained a hundred women/ Just to kill an unborn child", always being used to substantiate this. However, extensive research suggests this song is actually about the demise of the hedonism of the 1960s. The "man of energy" referred to is Charles Manson and the "unborn child" is Sharon Tate's unborn baby when the Manson "Family" committed the atrocities in 1969.

In "The Land of Plenty", he characterizes the United States (if not the opulent West in general) of benightedness: "May the lights in The Land of Plenty/ Shine on the truth some day".

War is an enduring theme of Cohen's work which in his earlier songs, as indeed in his early life, he approached ambivalently. Challenged in 1974 over his serious demeanor in concerts and the military salutes with which he ended them, Cohen remarked: "I sing serious songs, and I'm serious onstage because I couldn't do it any other way.... I don't consider myself a civilian. I consider myself a soldier, and that's the way soldiers salute". In "Field Commander Cohen" he imagines himself (perhaps metaphorically) as a soldier/ spy socializing with Fidel Castro in Cuba—where he had actually lived at the height of US-Cuba tensions in 1961, allegedly sporting a Che Guevara-style beard and military fatigues. This song was actually written immediately following Cohen's front-line stint with the Israeli air force, the "fighting in Egypt" documented in an (again perhaps metaphorical) passage of "Night Comes On". In 1973, Cohen, who had traveled to Jerusalem to sign up on the Israeli side in the Yom Kippur War, had instead been assigned to a USO-style entertainer tour of front-line tank emplacements in the Sinai Desert, coming under fire. A poetic mention of then-General Ariel Sharon delivered in the same mode as his Fidel Castro allusions, has given birth to the legend that Cohen and Sharon shared cognac together during Cohen's term in the Sinai.

Deeply moved by encounters with both Israeli and Arab soldiers, he left the country to write "Lover Lover Lover", which has often been interpreted as a personal renunciation of any part in such conflict, nonetheless ending with the hope his song will serve an unspecified listener as "a shield against the enemy". He would later remark, "'Lover, Lover, Lover' was born over there; The whole world has its eyes riveted on this tragic and complex conflict. Then again, I am faithful to certain ideas, inevitably. I hope that those of which I am in favour will gain." Asked which side he supported in the Arab-Israeli conflict, Cohen has responded: " I don't want to speak of wars or sides... Personal process is one thing, it's blood, it's the identification one feels with their roots and their origins. The militarism I practice as a person and a writer is another thing.... I don't wish to speak about war."

His recent politics continue a lifelong predilection for the underdog, the "beautiful loser". Whether recording "The Partisan", a French Resistance song by Anna Marly and Emmanuel d'Astier, or singing his own "The Old Revolution", written from the point of view of a defeated royalist, he has throughout his career through his music expressed his sympathy and support for the oppressed. Although Cohen's fascination with war is often as metaphor for more explicitly cultural and personal issues, as in *New Skin for the Old Ceremony*, by this measure his most "militant" album.

Cohen blends a good deal of pessimism about political/cultural issues with a great deal of humour and (especially in his later work) gentle acceptance. His wit contends with his stark analyses, as his songs are often verbally playful and even cheerful: In "Tower of Song", the famously raw-voiced Cohen sings ironically that he was "... born with the gift/ Of a golden voice"; the generally dark "Is This What You Wanted?" nonetheless contains playful lines "You were the whore and the beast of Babylon/ I was Rin Tin Tin"; in concert, he often plays around with his lyrics (for example, "If you want a doctor/ I'll examine every inch of you" from "I'm Your Man" will become "If you want a Jewish doctor ..."); and he will introduce one song by using a phrase from another song or poem (for example, introducing "Leaving Green Sleeves" by paraphrasing his own "Queen Victoria": "This is a song for those who are not nourished by modern love").

Cohen has also recorded such love songs as Irving Berlin's "Always" or the more obscure soul number "Be for Real" (originally sung by Marlena Shaw), chosen in part for their unlikely juxtaposition to his own work.

18

Writings of Farley Mowat

Farley McGill Mowat, (born May 12, 1921 in Belleville, Ontario) is a conservationist and one of Canada's most widely-read authors. Many of his most popular works have been memoirs of his childhood, his war service, and his work as a naturalist. His works have been translated into 52 languages and he has sold more than 14 million books. He achieved fame with the publication of his books on the Canadian North, such as *People of the Deer* (1952) and *Never Cry Wolf,* (1963). The latter, an account of his experiences with wolves in the Arctic, was made into a film, released in 1983.

Mowat's advocacy for environmental causes, and a writing style that "never let[s] the facts get in the way of the truth," have earned him both praise and criticism: "few readers remain neutral." Nevertheless, his influence is undeniable: *Never Cry Wolf* is credited with shifting the mythology and fear of wolves. His stories are fast-paced, gripping, personal, and conversational. Descriptions of Mowat refer to his "commitment to ideals," "poetic descriptions and vivid images," but also to his strong antipathies, which provoke "ridicule, lampoons and at times, evangelical condemnation."

Childhood

Great grandnephew of Ontario premier Sir Oliver Mowat, Farley Mowat was born in 1921 in Belleville, Ontario and grew up in Richmond Hill, Ontario where he attended Richmond Hill High School. His father, Angus Mowat, had fought at the Battle of Vimy Ridge, became a librarian, and enjoyed minor success as a novelist. Farley began writing informally while his family lived in Windsor from 1930–1933.

At the height of the Great Depression, the family relocated to Saskatoon, Saskatchewan. As a boy, Mowat was fascinated by nature and animals. With his dog, Mutt (the hero of *The Dog Who Wouldn't Be,* 1957), Mowat explored the Saskatchewan countryside. He also kept a rattlesnake, a squirrel, two owls (*Owls in the Family* 1962), a Florida alligator, several cats, and hundreds of insects as pets. With some of his friends, Mowat created the Beaver Club of Amateur Naturalists, and kept a museum in the Mowat basement, which included the joined skull of a two-headed calf, some stuffed birds, and a bear cub. This museum eventually had to be moved after an invasion by moths and beetles.

At the age of 13, Mowat founded a nature newsletter, *Nature Lore,* and had a weekly column on birds in the Saskatoon *Star-Phoenix*. He used the money he gained from his writing to feed ducks and geese who would have otherwise died because they didn't migrate south for the winter. His friends were children at the Dundurn Indian Reserve. In 1935, at age 15, Mowat made his first trip to the Arctic with his great-uncle Frank, an amateur birder.

War Service

During the Second World War, Mowat was commissioned as a Second Lieutenant into the Second Battalion, Hastings and Prince Edwards Regiment, affectionately known as the *Hasty Ps*. He later went overseas as a reinforcement officer for that regiment, joining the Canadian Army in the United Kingdom. On 10 July 1943, he was a subaltern in command of a rifle platoon, and participated in the initial landings of Operation Husky, the Allied invasion of Sicily.

Mowat served throughout the campaign as a platoon commander, and moved to Italy in September 1943, seeing further combat until December 1943. During the Moro River Campaign, he suffered from battle stress, heightened after an incident on Christmas Day outside of Ortona, Italy when he was left weeping at the feet of an unconscious friend, Major Alex Campbell, who had an enemy bullet in his head. He then accepted a job as Intelligence Officer at battalion headquarters, later moving to Brigade Headquarters. He stayed in Italy as a D-Day Dodger in the 1st Canadian Infantry Division for most of the war, eventually being promoted to the rank of captain.

He moved with the Division to Northwest Europe in early 1945. There, he worked as an intelligence agent in The Netherlands and went through enemy lines to start unofficial negotiations about food drops with General Blaskowitz. The food drops, under the codename Operation Manna, saved thousands of Dutch lives.

He also formed the 1st Canadian Army Museum Collection Team, according to his book *My Father's Son,* and arranged for the transport to Canada of several tons of German military equipment, including a V2 rocket and several armoured vehicles. (It is believed that some of these vehicles are on display today at the Canadian Forces Base Borden tank museum.)

Mowat was discharged at the conclusion of the Second World War in 1945 as a Captain, and was considered for promotion to Major, though he turned down the offer as it was incumbent on him volunteering to stay in the military until "no longer needed", which Mowat assumed to mean duty with the Canadian Army Occupation Force (CAOF) but might also have meant the conclusion of the war with Japan.

Literary Career

Returning to Canada after the war, Mowat studied biology at the University of Toronto. During a field trip to Northern Canada, Mowat became outraged at the plight of the Ihalmiut, a Caribou Inuit band, which he attributed to misunderstanding by whites. His outrage led him to publish his first novel, *People of the Deer* (1952). This book made Mowat into a literary celebrity and contributed to the shift in the Canadian government's Inuit policy: the government began shipping meat and dry goods to a people they previously denied existed.

This work was followed by a Governor General's Award-winning children's book, *Lost in the Barrens* (1956), which was about two teenagers — one white, one Cree — lost in the Arctic. The children are able to combine their skills to survive for part of the winter, but ultimately, they almost die before being saved by an Inuit boy whose knowledge of the Arctic supplements their skills.

Mowat followed up these works with a series of personal memoirs. *The Regiment* (1955) is a skillful and – unusual for military regimental histories of that era – highly readable account of the regiment he had served in during the Second World War. The Dog Who Wouldn't Be *(1957) and* Owls in the Family *(1961) are humorous memoirs about his childhood.*

During this period, Mowat also wrote two non-fiction accounts of the exploits of salvage tugs belonging to Foundation Maritime. The first, *The Grey Seas Under* (1958), chronicles the career of the tug Foundation Franklin, and the second, *The Serpent's Coil* (1961), chronicles the rescue of the British freighter *Leicester* in the face of two hurricanes by the tugs *Foundation Josephine* and *Foundation Lillian.*

In 1963, Mowat wrote a possibly fictionalised account of his experiences in the Canadian Arctic with Arctic wolves entitled *Never Cry Wolf,* which is thought to have been instrumental in changing popular attitudes on the canids. The work and its claims has been criticised.

Mowat then went through a phase of being very interested in Viking voyages to Canada, which resulted in the books *West-Viking* (1965), a controversial and largely debunked analysis of the Norse sagas trying to pin their accounts to specific Canadian geography, and *The Curse of the Viking Grave* (1968).

Mowat then moved to Burgeo, Newfoundland, where he lived for 8 years. He published three books describing his evolving view of his Newfoundland neighbours: in *The Rock Within the Sea* (1968), he presents Newfoundlanders as a heroic people uncorrupted by modern technology; *The Boat Who Wouldn't Float* (1969) reflects his disillusionment with a few Newfoundlanders; and, completing his disillusionment, *A Whale for the Killing* (1972) presents the shooting of a trapped and doomed whale as an inhumane tragedy. He was also co-author for the 1981 film version with Peter Strauss and Richard Widmark.

Mowat published a denunciation of "the destruction of animal life in the north Atlantic" entitled *Sea of Slaughter* in 1984. In 1985, as a part of the promotional tour for this book, Mowat accepted an invitation to speak at a university in Chico, California. However, U.S. customs officials at Lester B. Pearson International Airport in Toronto denied Mowat entry to the United States. They wouldn't tell him why specifically, but did tell him that it was because of a security file about him that indicated he should be denied entry "for violating any one of 33 statutes" (which ranged from being a member of the Communist Party to being a member of several other radical groups). The result was a media circus, which brought worldwide attention to Mowat. The negative publicity eventually forced the Reagan Administration to decide that Mowat was free to visit the U.S., but Mowat, peeved by being initially refused, declined. Mowat speculated on the reasons why he was refused entry to the U.S. in his 1985 book, *My Discovery of America*.

Then, Mowat became very interested in Dian Fossey, the American ethologist who studied gorillas and who was brutally murdered in Rwanda in 1985. Mowat published two books about Fossey: *Virunga: The Passion of Dian Fossey* (1987) and *Woman in the Mists* (1987).

In the 1990s and 2000s, Mowat's works have mainly consisted of recombinations of themes he had previously dealt with. He returns to his World War II military service in *My Father's Son* (1992), and to his childhood in *Born Naked* (1993). He returns to the Canadian Arctic in *High Latitudes: An Arctic Journey* (2002) (an account of a 1966 trek in northern Canada) and *No Man's River* (2004) (an account of an Arctic adventure he took amongst the Ihalmiut in 1947). In *Rescue the Earth: Conversations* (1990), Mowat continued his work as an environmental advocate. In *The Farfarers* (2000), Mowat returned to the theme of pre-Columbian interactions between Europe and North America. In *Bay of Spirits: A Love Story* (2006) he returns to stories from his travels to St. Pierre and the southwest coast of Newfoundland in the early 1960s. These events have already led to *This Rock Within the Sea: A Heritage Lost* (1968), *The Boat Who Wouldn't Float* (1969), and *A Whale for the Killing* (1972). However, the 2006 effort adds many new personal details as well as fresh accounts of sailing the southwest coast and meeting its inhabitants that were not included in the previous works from this time period in his life.

He and his wife Claire currently live in Port Hope, Ontario. They spend their summers on a farm in Cape Breton, Nova Scotia.

Criticism

The *Toronto Star* has written that Mowat's memoirs are at least partially fictional. In a 1968 interview with CBC Radio, Farley admitted that he doesn't let the facts get in the way of the truth (*Canada Reads*). Once, when Mowat said that he had spent two summers and a winter studying wolves, the *Toronto Star* wrote that Mowat had only spent 90 hours studying the wolves.

A not-unbiased article by John Goddard in the May 1996 issue of *Saturday Night* lays out a somewhat more in-depth criticism of Farley's celebrated works, especially *Never Cry Wolf.* In his article, "A Real Whopper," he purported to poke many holes in Mowat's claim that the book was non-fictional. He wrote, "As for the authenticity of his wolf story, he virtually abandoned his wolf-den observations after less than four weeks." Mowat denied Goddard's criticisms but allegedly did not refute specific accusations. Canadian Wildlife Federation official Frank Banfield, in a 1964 article published in the *Canadian Field-Naturalist,* compared Mowat's 1963 bestseller to Little Red Riding Hood, stating, "I hope that readers of "Never Cry Wolf" will realize that both stories have about the same factual content." L. David Mech, a wolf expert, stated that Mowat is no scientist and that in all his studies, he had never encountered a wolf pack which primarily subsisted on small prey as shown in Mowat's book.

19

Writings of Timothy Findley

Timothy Irving Frederick Findley, (October 30, 1930-June 21, 2002) was a Canadian novelist and playwright. He was also informally known by the nickname Tiff or Tiffy, an acronym of his initials.

One of three sons, Findley was born in Toronto, Ontario, to Allan Gilmour Findley, a stockbroker, and his wife, the former Margaret Maude Bull. His paternal grandfather was president of Massey-Harris, the farm-machinery company. He was raised in the upper class Rosedale district of the city, attending boarding school at St. Andrew's College (although leaving during grade 10 for health reasons). He pursued a career in the arts, studying dance and acting, and had significant success as an actor before turning to writing. He was part of the original Stratford Festival company in the 1950s, acting alongside Alec Guinness, and appeared in the first production of Thornton Wilder's *The Matchmaker* at the Edinburgh Festival. He also played Peter Pupkin in the CBC Television adaptation of Stephen Leacock's *Sunshine Sketches of a Little Town* in 1952, and had an uncredited (and unconfirmed) minor role in the 1964 television film *John Cabot: A Man of the Renaissance.*

Though Findley had declared his homosexuality as a teenager, he married actress/photographer Janet Reid (born 1930) in 1959, but the union lasted only three months and was dissolved by divorce or annulment two years later. Eventually he became the domestic partner of writer William Whitehead, whom he met in 1962, either while working as an arts reporter for the Canadian Broadcast Corporation or while appearing in a theatre production (sources differ). Findley and Whitehead also collaborated on several documentary projects in the 1970s.

Through Wilder, Findley became a close friend of actress Ruth Gordon, whose work as a screenwriter and playwright inspired Findley to consider writing as well. After Findley published his first short story in the *Tamarack Review*, Gordon encouraged him to pursue writing more actively, and he eventually left acting in the 1960s.

Findley's first two novels, *The Last of the Crazy People* (1967) and *The Butterfly Plague* (1969), were originally published in Britain and the United States after having been rejected by Canadian publishers. Findley's third novel, *The Wars*, was published to great acclaim in 1977 and went on to win the Governor General's Award for fiction. It was adapted for film in 1981.

Timothy Findley received a Governor General's Award, the Canadian Authors Association Award, an ACTRA Award, the Order of Ontario, the Ontario Trillium Award, and in 1985 he was appointed an Officer of the Order of Canada. He was a founding member and chair of the Writers' Union of Canada, and a president of the Canadian chapter of PEN International.

His writing, typical of the Southern Ontario Gothic genre, was heavily influenced by Jungian psychology, and mental illness, gender and sexuality were frequent recurring themes in his work. His characters often carried dark personal secrets, and were often conflicted — sometimes to the point of psychosis — by these burdens.

He publicly mentioned his homosexuality, passingly and perhaps for the first time, on a broadcast of the programme *The Shulman File* in the 1970s, taking flabberghasted host Morton Shulman completely by surprise. Shulman was a man who did not rattle easily.

Findley and Whitehead resided at Stone Orchard, a farm near Cannington, Ontario, and in the south of France. In 1996, Findley was honoured by the French government, who declared him a Chevalier de l'Ordre des arts et des lettres.

Findley was also the author of several dramas for television and stage. *Elizabeth Rex,* his most successful play, premiered at the Stratford Festival of Canada to rave reviews and won a Governor General's award. *Shadows,* first performed in 2001, was his last completed work. Findley was also an active mentor to a number of young Canadian writers, including Marnie Woodrow and Elizabeth Ruth.

In October 2001 when, as writer-in-residence at the University of Calgary, he gave a talk in which he compared oil companies to the terrorists who attacked the World Trade Center the month before. He said the oil companies are doing little to reduce greenhouse gases and they rush to exploit global gas and petroleum reserves. "What's going to happen in the future if we allow corporate profits to prevail above all other concerns?" Findley asked. "Talk about suicide bombers and all the innocent others who die along with them.... Think about that (corporate profits) and consider the future of our children, our country and our civilization."

In the final years of Findley's life, declining health led him to move his Canadian residence to Toronto, and Stone Orchard was purchased by Canadian dancer Rex Harrington.

Not Wanted on the Voyage

Not Wanted on the Voyage is a novel by Canadian author Timothy Findley, which presents a magic realist post-modern re-telling of the Great Flood in the biblical Book of Genesis. It was first published by Viking Canada in the autumn of 1984.

Noah Noyes, an authoritarian doctor and father whose obsession with God's law leads him to neglect his family, his wife, Mrs. Noyes, an alcoholic who talks to animals, and Mottyl, her blind cat are the central characters of the novel. Noah and Mrs. Noyes have three sons, Shem, Japeth, and Ham. Shem is married to Hannah, who spends a great deal of time with Dr. Noyes. Japeth is married to Emma, a young girl of about 12, who refuses to consummate their marriage.

One day, an exhausted Yaweh visits Dr. Noyes. Yaweh is depressed to the point of willfully allowing himself to die, due to the treatment he's received from humanity. He tells the Noyes that the people of the City threw offal, rotten fruit, and feces at his carriage and has assassinated him 7 times. Yaweh remains depressed until he's inspired by a magic show Noah puts on to raise his spirits. Noah puts a penny under a glass bottle then fills the bottle with water. Due to refraction of the penny's image, the coin appears to vanish, but Yaweh becomes obsessed by the idea that the application of water can make things disappear.

Soon Yaweh tells Noah to build an ark in preparation for the flood. Noah is resolutely obedient, but some in his family react negatively. Ham quickly marries Lucy, a mysterious seven-foot-tall woman with webbed fingers (a trait found only in angels, according to the novel) who is eventually revealed to be Lucifer in drag. As Yaweh leaves, Mottyl hears flies buzzing from within Yaweh's carriage and knows that Yaweh has resigned himself to death.

Noah is adamant that Yaweh's edict must be followed to the letter and insists that there must be only two of every animal. Mrs. Noyes tries to bring Mottyl, who Noah has decreed must stay behind since he's chosen Yaweh's own two pet cats to represent felines on the ark. Noah sets fire to the house and barn, with Mottyl inside, offering all their additional animals as a giant sacrifice to Yaweh. Mrs.

Noyes in enraged at the attempt to kill her cat, and by the carnage in what is left of her home, and refuses to board the ark. Noah is concerned that if Mrs. Noyes does not come, the ark and its passengers will be doomed, as Yaweh's edict clearly states that Noah's wife must be aboard. Mrs. Noyes hides in Noah's orchard as the rain starts, but leaves when she notices Emma's sister Lotte, a "monkey child" trying to cross the river. Mrs. Noyes rescues Lotte and agrees to board only if Lotte can also come. Noah agrees to let Lotte on board, but has Japeth kill her shortly after. Mrs. Noyes again rebels, but ultimately agrees to board the ark and smuggles Mottyl aboard, hidden in her apron.

As the voyage begins Noah quickly imposes his will on his family by drawing a line between the "rebellious" elements (Mrs. Noyes, Emma, Ham, and Lucy) and the rest (himself, Hannah, Japeth, and Shem). One day, dolphins swim by the ark, attempting to befriend the inhabitants. Noah decides that the dolphins must be pirates and has Japeth slaughter them. Mrs. Noyes attempts to stop him, and once the "pirates" have been defeated, Noah locks Mrs. Noyes, Lucy, Ham, and Emma in the lower levels of the ark, forcing them to care for the animals alone. Meanwhile, Noah, Hannah, Shem, and Japeth enjoy quarters on the deck of the ark and freedom from heavy chores.

Noah notices that Japeth is becoming more preoccupied with sex and often eyes Hannah in a way that makes Noah wary. He decides that the solution is to force Emma to consummate their marriage. Noah has Emma brought to the deck and "inspects" her to see what the problem is. He decides that Emma's "tightness" is the reason why Japeth could not "gain entry" and requests that the Unicorn is brought to aid the problem. Noah uses the Unicorn to "open" Emma for Japeth, a process which traumatizes Emma and severely injures the Unicorn. When Japeth finds out what his father has done, hecut off the Unicorn's horn. Emma is then forced to live on the top deck to be near her husband.

Mrs. Noyes, Lucy, and Ham decide to rebel against Noah and the others. They formulate a plan to burn through the locked door using the two demons on board. They get the door open and plan to close the armoury, where Japeth sleeps, from the outside so as to neutralize Japeth. Unfortunately, Japeth is patrolling the deck and captures the escapees. He ties up Mrs.

Noyes, Lucy, and Ham and throws the demons overboard, which enrages Lucy. She breaks free of her bonds and curses Japeth so that his wounds will never heal properly and he will always smell of the violence he has inflicted on others. Mrs. Noyes, Ham, and Lucy are locked below again, this time with boards and chains locking the door from the outside.

Lucy plans another escape and has Crow take a message to Emma to release them. Emma removes all the chains and bars while Noah and Hannah are preoccupied with praying, Shem is preoccupied with eating, and Japeth is preoccupied dressing his wounds. Mrs. Noyes, Lucy, and Ham bar the armoury and the chapel, locking in Noah, Hannah, and Japeth, but they are unable to find Shem.

While locked in the chapel, Hannah's labour begins. She asks Noah to call for help, but he refuses to call for anyone until the baby is born. Noah knows that the baby is likely his and is worried that it will be a "monkey child" like Lotte, as Japeth's dead twin brother was also monkey-like. When the baby is born dead it is indeed revealed to be a "monkey child." Ham, hearing Hannah's cries of pain, opens the chapel door to help Hannah. He is quickly brained by Shem, but not before he sees Hannah's child. Hannah wraps it in blankets to hide its hairy arms and throw the baby overboard.

A truce between the factions is tacity called. The weather is sunny for the first time since the start of the rain, and Noah asks Emma to send a dove to look for land. When the dove does not return, they continue to send birds until Noah decides to send his own trained dove. Noah's dove returns with an olive branch, which Noah uses to prove Yaweh's edict. The other members of the ark remain unconvinced, as they know it is the same branch from the dove's cage. The novel ends with Mrs. Noyes sitting on deck with Mottyl, praying to the clouds for rain.

The book is written by Timothy Findley and is produced by Penguin Books.

20

Writings of John Hugh MacLennan

John Hugh MacLennan, CC, CQ (March 20, 1907 - November 9, 1990) was a Canadian author and professor of English at McGill University. He won five Governor General's Awards and a Royal Bank Award.

Family and Childhood

MacLennan was born in Glace Bay, Nova Scotia on March 20, 1907. His parents were Dr. Samuel MacLennan, a colliery physician, and Katherine MacQuerrie; Hugh also had an older sister named Frances. Samuel was a stern Calvinist, while Katherine was creative, warm and dreamy, and both parents would be large influences on Hugh's character. In 1913, the family spent several months in London while Samuel took on further study to become a medical specialist. On returning to Canada, they briefly lived in Sydney, Nova Scotia before settling in Halifax. In December 1917, young Hugh experienced the Halifax Explosion, which he would later write about in his first published novel, *Barometer Rising*. From the ages of twelve to twenty-one, he slept in a tent in the family's backyard, even in the cold winter, possibly as an escape from his strict father. Hugh grew up believing in the importance of religion; he and Frances regularly went to Sunday School, and the family attended Presbyterian church services twice each Sunday. He was also active in sports, and became especially good at tennis, eventually winning the Nova Scotia men's double championship in 1927.

Education

MacLennan and his sister were pushed extremely hard by their father to spend long hours learning the Classics. While this was very difficult for Frances, who had no interest in Greek, Hugh grew to enjoy this field of study. Their father had an ambitious educational path planned for Hugh: studying the Classics at Dalhousie University, getting a Rhodes Scholarship, and then continuing his studies in England. MacLennan received top marks at Dalhousie and succeeded in winning a Rhodes Scholarship, allowing him to go on to Oxford University.

While at Dalhousie, he realized that his inner wish was to pursue an artistic career, the influence of his creative mother. At Oxford, he struggled with balancing his passion for Greek and Latin studies with these artistic instincts. In his first year, MacLennan worked incredibly hard at his Classics courses, but was only able to achieve second-class. By his second year, he had resolved himself to such results, and while still working diligently, decided not to overwork himself as before. In his fourth year, he was finding it increasingly difficult to concentrate on his studies, and spent more and more time at tennis and writing poetry. In letters to his family from around this time are hints that he hoped to be a successful writer. In late 1931, MacLennan sent some of his poetry to three publishers, including the firms of John Lane and Elkin Mathews, but it was turned down.

MacLennan's four years in Oxford gave him the opportunity to travel throughout Europe, and he visited countries such as Switzerland, France, Greece and Italy. He spent some of his holidays lodging with a family in Germany, through which he acquired a very good proficiency in German. His travels and his exposure to different political ideas caused MacLennan to begin to question his father's puritanical, Conservative attitudes that he had until then taken for granted.

MacLennan won a $400 scholarship to continue his studies at Princeton University, and despite his growing disinclination to keep studying the Classics, he decided to go there. This was partly to appease his father, and partly because the depression meant that there were few jobs available. In June 1932, while sailing home from England, he met his future wife, American Dorothy Duncan. Falling in love with her made him change his mind about Princeton. For one thing, his father insisted he should not get married before becoming financially independent, which would mean delaying marriage at least until his graduation. In addition, MacLennan was already unhappy about having to accept money from his father for the part of his Princeton studies that would not be covered by his scholarship. However, his applications were rejected from both of the Canadian universities he applied to that had Classics Department positions opening; thus, he grudgingly agreed to go to Princeton after all.

His three years at Princeton were unhappy. The style of classical study there was very different from what he was used to at Oxford, with Princeton's scholarship "consist[ing] of extremely detailed analyses of classical texts and sources—thorough, but unoriginal." He began to rebel against his father's ideals: he stopped going to church and put increasing energy into his writing at the expense of his studies; furthermore, in addition to resenting his financial dependence on his father, he continued his relationship with Dorothy even though he knew his father would not approve of her American, Lowland Scottish, Christian Science, business-world background. During this time, MacLennan also began to be influenced by Marxism.

Unpublished Novels

At Princeton, MacLennan wrote his first novel, *So All Their Praises*. He found one publisher who was willing to take the manuscript, as long as he made certain changes; however, this company went out of business before the book could be published. In spring 1935, he finished his PhD thesis, *Oxyrhynchus: An Economic and Social Study*, about the decline of a Roman colony in Egypt, which was published by Princeton University Press and reprinted in 1968 by A.M. Hakkert.

In 1935, the depression resulted in there being very few teaching jobs available, and MacLennan's field of study, the Classics, was in particular becoming less significant in North American education. He took a position at Lower Canada College in Montreal, even though he felt it was beneath him, as just his Dalhousie BA would have been a sufficient qualification for the job. He generally did not enjoy working there, and resented the long hours required of him for low pay, but was nonetheless a stimulating teacher, at least for the brighter students. MacLennan would later poke fun at Lower Canada College in his depiction of Waterloo School in *The Watch That Ends the Night.* On June 22, 1936, he and Dorothy were wed near her home in Wilmette, Illinois, and settled in Montreal.

Meanwhile, in 1934–1938, MacLennan was working on his second novel, *A Man Should Rejoice.* Longman, Green and Company and Duell, Sloan and Pearce both showed strong interest in the novel, but in the end neither published it.

In February 1939, MacLennan's father died after suffering from high blood pressure. It was a huge shock to MacLennan, as in the previous year they had just begun to become closer and to reconcile their opposing views. For several months after his father's death MacLennan continued to write letters to him, in which he discussed his thoughts on the possibility and implications of a war in Europe.

Barometer Rising

Dorothy convinced MacLennan that the failure of his first two novels was he had set one in Europe and the other in U.S.A; she persuaded him to write about Canada, the country he knew best. She told him that "Nobody's going to understand Canada until she evolves a literature of her own, and you're the fellow to start bringing Canadian novels up to date." Until then there had been no real tradition of Canadian literature, and MacLennan set out to define Canada for Canadians through a national novel.

Barometer Rising, his novel about the social class structure of Nova Scotia and the Halifax Explosion of 1917, was published in 1941.

Later Novels

His most famous novel, *Two Solitudes*, a literary allegory for the tensions between English and French Canada, followed in 1945. That year, he left Lower Canada College. *Two Solitudes* won MacLennan his first Governor General's Award for Fiction.

In 1948, MacLennan published *The Precipice*, which again won the Governor General's Award. The following year, he published a collection of essays, *Cross Country*, which won the Governor General's Award for Non-Fiction.

In 1951, MacLennan returned to teaching, accepting a position at McGill University. In 1954, he published another essay collection, *Thirty and Three*, which again won the Governor General's Award for Non-Fiction.

One of MacLennan's students at McGill was Marian Engel, who became a noted Canadian novelist in the 1970s. Another notable student was Leonard Cohen, the popular songwriter, poet and novelist.

Duncan died in 1957. MacLennan married his second wife, Aline Walker, in 1959. That same year, he published *The Watch That Ends the Night*, which won his final Governor General's Award. In 1967, he was made a Companion of the Order of Canada. In 1985 he was made a Knight of the National Order of Quebec.

MacLennan continued to write and publish work, with his final novel *Voices in Time* appearing in 1980. He died in Montreal, Quebec. The Canadian band The Tragically Hip, on their album *Fully Completely*, have a song called "Courage (for Hugh MacLennan)". A passage from *The Watch That Ends the Night* is adapted for use in the songlink title.

21

Life and Works of Susanna Moodie

Susanna Moodie, born Strickland (6 December 1803 – 8 April 1885) was a British born Canadian author who wrote about her experiences as a settler in Canada.

Biography

Prior to her marriage and emigration to Canada in 1832, Susanna Moodie wrote for the Anti-Slavery Society. During this period she produced the two antislavery tracts, "The History of Mary Prince, a West Indian Slave" (1831) and "Negro Slavery Described by a Negro" (1831). Along with her other sisters, Susanna grew up appreciating literature, recognizing its value for the family's betterment. She demonstrated a forward-thinking mind in her approach to life which helped her greatly when she left England.

Upon arriving in Canada, the couple took advantage of the land grant system and quickly secured land for clearing to try their hand at farming. Like many newcomers, they had been told that after receiving free land, they could grow and sell produce and perhaps keep a few animals. They decided on land with a house on the property and agreed with the previous tenants to take possession of the house.

Delays from the residents forced the Moodies to buy a hut on the property and the date to move in dragged on for many months. The tenants refused to leave the property, among the excuses were the approaching winter season and that the wife was expecting a child. The Moodies paid a high price for the hut situated on the property and suffered great inconvenience as a result of living in the shanty with few comforts and many deficiencies. It was not until the following summer that the premises were vacated but not before they left the home in a shambles, with water damage, dirt and dead animals left behind for them to clean. In spite of this, the Moodies were relieved to finally move in and quickly set out to clean it and fix the damage.

Susanna admitted in *Roughing it in the Bush* that she came to Canada expressly because of the "promise of a large grant of land, and the false statement we heard regarding it." This realization forced her to realize how much more difficult it would be to succeed in the new country. She also had to confront attitudes toward class which she brought from the old country. Many were the times that she did not comprehend the people and was, in turn, misunderstood and thought of as feeling superior to those around her. People already settled and suffering from a poor economy viewed the bright- eyed, uninformed newcomers with contempt.

Once the young family moved into their home, the industrious couple plunged into different ventures. Susanna started gardening and Mr. Moodie became involved in a scheme to set up farming upon shares. The idea was for partners to share the fruits and labour of a farm for profit. Sadly, the venture was unsuccessful and the partners stole much of the

Moodies' harvest. The Moodies' inexperience guaranteed that they would be taken advantage of. The 12-month agreement with the partners taught the Moodies a lesson which Susanna would later write about in *Roughing It in the Bush* advising new emigrants against falling into such traps.

Realizing that the farm and property were draining their resources, they decided to sell their little farm and Mrs. Moodie wrote: "When our resolution was formed to ... take up our grant of land in the backwoods no one was so earnest in trying to persuade us to give up the ruinous scheme as our friend Brian B. who became quite eloquent in his description of the trials and sorrows that awaited us..." *(pg 159). Susanna, however did not dwell on the negative for long, and soon realized how emigration could be a wonderful opportunity if one worked hard and possessed the means and determination required to succeed.

Among other setbacks that the Moodies suffered was a failed boat venture which did not produce a profit. The family was not able to recover fully from this investment. Each failure filled the Moodies with regret for the financial errors made due to their lack of knowledge of the new country and its practices.

After leaving their farm, the Moodie family decided to move into the woods where Susanna's siblings, Catharine and Samuel, resided. They journeyed with the children and all their belongings, and hired 2 men to take them to their property. The voyage was not without accidents and many of their belongings were damaged, but the family arrived and made arrangements to stay at her sister Traill's place with their long journey ending with the very affectionate welcome Catharine gave them. Originally, the Moodies had planned to stay with Samuel, but since his wife was away at the time, they were sent to Catharine's place where they could rest assured that all comforts of the humble dwelling would gladly be offered up to the tired travellers.

Once the family settled on their own land, they began life anew and quickly adapted to the new surroundings and challenges of the territory. They built their log house and cleared land to give it another try. Their interaction and friendship with the Indians of the area, along with their respect and affection for them, is evident in *Roughing it in the Bush* where Susanna wrote: "... and as my husband never allowed them to eat with the servants, but brought them to his own table, they soon grew friendly and communicative..."

It was this attitude of interest and respect that earned the Moodies the affection of many neighbours in the backwoods and Indians of the area. In her book she described them with great admiration. She wrote of how the Indian families behaved and lived, "the affection of Indian parents to their children, and deference which they pay to the aged, is a beautiful and touching trait in their character. *Roughing it in the Bush*. She dealt with them extensively and marvelled at their great sense of humour. She also described the practice of the 'bees' among the neighbours which she perceived as useful but draining on resources of the host family, with the Moodies participating on many occasions to erect homes, clear land and help those around them.

With time, that resilience grew to a stronger emotion for her adopted country. On a trip to Stoney

Lake< with her husband near Clear Lake and Sandy Point, she wrote: "In moments like these, I ceased to regret my separation from my native land; and filled with the love of Nature my heart forgot for the time, the love of home..." *Roughing it in the Bush*.

As true bush people, the young family had few visitors and thus, did not miss material goods until the lack was noted by visitors. In 1836, the Moodies were taken advantage of by a man that John met on a train. Moodie befriended him and the man soon arrived at their home and stayed for 9 months. In *Roughing it in the Bush* she wrote: "For the first time I felt heartily ashamed of our humble fare." Unfortunately, the experience was most unpleasant for Susanna. The man mistreated her terribly and did not leave until the Moodies' patience was finally spent and he was asked outright to leave their home.

Tragedy struck a year later when the Moodie home suffered a big fire which was caused by the inexperience of one of the maids. Susanna who was alone with her children at the time, managed to salvage some items but much was lost and they were forced, once again, to rely on Catharine Parr Traill's kindness until repairs could be arranged.

Although the young family had few resources and suffered from many privations, most of the time, they are able to employ others to help them. They hired help for the farm, child-care and house-work. They did so, perhaps in an effort to maintain to the level of life to which they were accustomed back home. The expenses of hiring others did have consequences, however, and they were indebted for most of their lives. The Moodies were likely perceived by others as more fortunate than those who had to learn to work on their own and master tasks they had never done before but they were also appreciated for their positive and helpful attitude in the bush.

On one occasion, Mr. Moodie broke his leg, leaving Susanna completely demoralized when she realized that the doctor would not go out to their log house. This situation was not uncommon for families in the backwoods and she wrote in desperation: "Perhaps he did not like to incur the expense of a fatiguing journey with small chance of obtaining a sufficient remuneration." *Roughing it in the Bush.* Such was the lonely and hard life of the settler.

Around 1837 with the Rebellion, Mr. Moodie, along with Mr. Traill and Mr. Strickland, was called to military duty. When he heard of the burning of Toronto he immediately left in spite of his leg injury and Susanna found herself very lonely once again. Little news ever arrived in the bush and she admitted that "the honest backwoodsmen, perfectly ignorant of the abuses that had led to the present position of things, regarded the rebels as a set of monsters,..., and obeyed the call to arms with enthusiasm." *Roughing it in the Bush,* a circumstance which separated many a family, including the Moodies.

Although she felt the absence of her husband, she was also grateful for the salary he received with the rank of Captain. With money received from his service, the family was able to repay some debts and enjoy more peace of mind. It was at that time that Susanna was invited to write for "The Literary Garland" and was given the chance to earn some money for her family. She had been forced to decline many earlier requests for her work from American publications due to lack of funds for postage.

Susanna relished the $20 she received from her work for the Montreal publication and she felt a great satisfaction in being able to contribute to her family's welfare. Other ways with which she supplemented her income were by selling her paintings of birds and butterflies. Her brother Samuel Strickland even helped by selling many of them to soldiers who bought them without knowing who the painter was.

Foreseeing that the end of the war would leave her husband unemployed again, Susanna demonstrated her survival skills by writing to the Governor and asking him to employ her husband longer in order to avoid poverty for the family. Her brother-in-law, Mr. Traill, read the letter and took it to the post-office himself. She received no reply to or acknowledgement of her request and soon she began to prepare for the hard times ahead. Great was her surprise when the letter paid off and her husband was appointed paymaster to the militia, with the rank and full pay of Captain.

Slowly, many settlers and pioneers started to leave the backwoods for better prospects in the big cities. Her sister Catharine, as well as several friends, decided to move out of the backwoods and try their luck in more populated areas where work and opportunities were easier to come by. Once more Susanna was left alone, deeply feeling the loss of her allies in the bush.

The family's luck was once again turned [in 1839], when Mr. Moodie was offered the situation of Sheriff of Hastings County. The promotion helped the family repay debts and enjoy a security which had eluded them since their emigration. It also caused them to move to Belleville.

From 1847 to 1848, both Susanna and her husband edited and wrote for "Victoria Magazine." In 1852, she published *Roughing it in the Bush* which is her best known literary work. The books to follow included *Life in the Clearings,* published in 1853, and *Flora Lyndsay,* published in 1854.

Through the years Susanna never neglected her family back in England and she corresponded often with them and her old friends back home. She always expressed a warm relationship for those she left behind. She also understood very well, that under her circumstances and financial situation, she would most likely never see them again and instead, rejoiced at having two siblings so near and dear to her in Canada. To their credit John and Susanna exhibited great resilience and courage in trying new avenues to earn an income in spite of the setbacks. However, Susanna never really became content with her situation nor acclimatized to the *mores* of her new land.

She served as an anchor for her family and her long life drew her close to her children. Susanna developed a very strong relationship with her daughter Kate which intensified after John's death. Two of her sons, Dunbar and Donald, eventually moved to the United States. Susanna Moodie stayed in Belleville while her husband was alive. After his death in 1869, she moved to the Toronto area where she remained until her death, April 8, 1885.

Literarary Career

Susanna Moodie embraced the ability to relate her experiences in the bush as a duty to warn others from going to Canada without first reflecting on the wisdom of throwing away all the comforts of home for life in the bush. Although her story of the seven years she spent in the backwoods was told without overtly expressing regret for having left England, she acknowledged, after those years of hardship, that maybe gentlemen and women were less suited for that harsh life than they were lead to believe when enticed with free land grants in the new colony. The tone of her famous book, *Roughing it in the Bush,* belies her openness of mind with which she accepts all that her new life presents her.

The emigration to Canada meant times of great difficulty for the Moodie family. Susanna talked in her book of their privations and how they suffered near starvation and eventually had to ask neighbours for help. The good people in the bush, also suffering from deficiencies, offered assistance.

One such episode in her book told of the custom everyone has of borrowing from each other during the hard times in the backwoods. Times were often desperate and she described how on many occasions others borrowed from her, with or without her consent. She was struck by the boldness of many in taking what they needed or in asking for things they never meant to return. Mrs. Moodie herself tried not to borrow from those around her except for the very rare times when she could not help it. And she wrote of how oftentimes neighbours would borrow items and not reciprocate when she needed help.

She wrote of the numerous times that people tried to warn them: "... but it is not long that you will remain here... I never saw a gentleman from the old country make a good Canadian farmer... you will become a confirmed drunkard like the rest" *Roughing it in the Bush* and she recalled the feeling of dread over such forecasts.She felt close to nature in lieu of having people around her. In this state of mind of being homesick and lonely, Susanna recognized that people in Canada her native home. She often commented on how Canadians and Yankees did things differently. For example, she received negative comments on the fact that the Moodie family did not take their meals with the servants. She was similarly criticized for believing that poorer, uneducated people did not treat the privileged with sufficient deference. Susanna Moodie often felt isolated and lonely as would any settler in a new country. But because she retained a strong sense of class, she tended to attribute her feelings of isolation to her perception that her neighbours resented her status.

She enjoyed very much her interaction with Native Peoples: their exchanges, bartering, and many visits and meals and nights spent sharing each others' hospitality.

With adaptation Susanna came to terms with her homesickness and accepted that the custom of calling on friends and neighbours was practiced considerably less than she would have liked. She conceded that Canadians had many capabilities and talents and are a practical people which "will render them second to no people in the world; and that period is not far distant." *Roughing it in the Bush.*

Susanna noted numerous interesting customs such as the famous Charivari custom prevalent in those parts at the time. She also described the well-known logging-bee. as: "noisy, riotous, drunken meetings, often terminating in violent quarrels, sometimes in bloodshed. *Roughing it in the Bush.*

Nearing the end of her time in the bush, after they finally decided, to leave, she said: "For 7 years I had lived out of the world entirely, my person had been rendered coarse by hard work and exposure to the weather. I looked double the age I really was... I clung to my solitude. I did not like to be dragged from it... that was the last night I spent in the bush- in the dear forest home which I had loved in spite of all the hardships which we had endured since we pitched our tent in the backwoods..." *Roughing it in the Bush.*

Roughing it in the Bush

Susanna Moodie embraced the ability to relate her experiences in the bush as a duty to warn others from going to Canada without first reflecting on the wisdom of throwing away all the comforts of home for life in the bush.

Although her story of the seven years she spent in the backwoods was told without overtly expressing regret for having left England, she acknowledged, after those years of hardship, that maybe gentlemen and women were less suited for that harsh life than they were lead to believe when enticed with free land grants in the new colony. The tone of her famous book, *Roughing it in the Bush,* belies her openness of mind with which she accepts all that her new life presents her.

The emigration to Canada meant times of great difficulty for the Moodie family. Susanna talked in her book of their privations and how they suffered near starvation and eventually had to ask neighbours for help. The good people in the bush, also suffering from deficiencies, offered assistance.

One such episode in her book told of the custom everyone has of borrowing from each other during the hard times in the backwoods. Times were often desperate and she described how on many occasions others borrowed from her, with or without her consent. She was struck by the boldness of many in taking what they needed or in asking for things they never meant to return. Mrs. Moodie herself tried not to borrow from those around her except for the very rare times when she could not help it. And she wrote of how oftentimes neighbours would borrow items and not reciprocate when she needed help.

She wrote of the numerous times that people tried to warn them: "... but it is not long that you will remain here... I never saw a gentleman from the old country make a good Canadian farmer... you will become a confirmed drunkard like the rest" *Roughing it in the Bush,* and she recalled the feeling of dread over such forecasts.

She felt close to nature in lieu of having people around her. In this state of mind of being homesick and lonely, Susanna recognized that people in Canada her native home. She often commented on how Canadians and Yankees did things differently. For example, she received negative comments on the fact that the Moodie family did not take their meals with the servants. She was similarly criticized for believing that poorer, uneducated people did not treat the privileged with sufficient deference. Susanna Moodie often felt isolated and lonely as would any settler in a new country. But because she retained a strong sense of class, she tended to attribute her feelings of isolation to her perception that her neighbours resented her status.

She enjoyed very much her interaction with Native Peoples: their exchanges, bartering, and many visits and meals and nights spent sharing each others' hospitality.

With adaptation Susanna came to terms with her homesickness and accepted that the custom of calling on friends and neighbours was practiced considerably less than she would have liked. She conceded that Canadians had many capabilities and talents and are a practical people which "will render them second to no people in the world; and that period is not far distant." *Roughing it in the Bush.*

Susanna Moodie was first and foremost a writer. She enjoyed writing and had an uncanny ear for accents and she transcribed what people said around her giving an amusing air to her anecdotes. She used many of her writings to offer practical advice and also enjoyed writing romantic stories. She was a talented painter of watercolours.>

Among Susanna's many interests were devising recipes for her growing family. She had many uses for dandelion root, especially as a drink. She learned that when destitute of animal foods, they could eat squirrels in pies, stews and roasts. To provide food, John and Susanna often fished at daybreak for 1 hour and had plenty of bass and "mukinongé" to eat.

The family maintained an active interest in practicing their religion with the few opportunities they found while they were in the bush. They developed an interest in spiritualism, especially after their son John's death.

22

Life and Works of Samuel Hearne

Samuel Hearne (1745-November 1792) was an explorer, fur-trader, author, and naturalist. He was the first European to make an overland excursion across northern Canada to the Arctic Ocean. In 1774 Hearne built Cumberland House for the Hudson's Bay Company, its first interior trading post and the first permanent settlement in present Saskatchewan.

Early Life

Samuel Hearne was born in 1745 in England. Hearne's father was a senior engineer of the London Bridge Water Works but he died in 1748. After some elementary education, Hearne joined the Royal Navy in 1756 as midshipman under the fighting captain Samuel Hood. He remained with Hood during the Seven Years' War, seeing considerable action during the conflict, including the bombardment of Le Havre. At the end of the Seven Years' War, having served in the English Channel and then the Mediterranean, he left the navy in 1763. His activities during the next three years are unknown.

In February 1766 he joined the Hudson's Bay Company as a mate on the sloop Churchill, which was then engaged in the Inuit trade out of Prince of Wales Fort, Churchill, Manitoba. Two years later he became mate on the brigantine Charlotte and participated in the company's short-lived black whale fishery. In 1768, he examined portions of the Hudson Bay coasts with a view to improving the cod fishery. During this time he gained a reputation for snowshoeing.

Hearne was able to improve his navigational skills by observing William Wales who was at Hudson Bay during 1768-1769 after being commissioned by the Royal Society to observe the Transit of Venus with Joseph Dymond. Wales later sailed with Captain James Cook on his second and third voyages.

Exploration

From 1769 to 1772, Hearne was employed in north-western discovery, searching especially for certain copper mines described by Indians as "Far-Away-Metal River". These copper mines were found in the Barren Lands where the ground is permanently frozen to within a few inches of the surface, creating, in many areas, vast stretches of mosquito- and fly-infested swamp during the summer thaw. For this reason it was decided that travel in winter was preferable.

His first attempt began on 6 November 1769. The large size of the expedition and too much European equipment being carried led to the desertion of his Indian guides and the failure of the expedition. His second, commencing 23 February 1770, failed because his quadrant was broken and much of his equipment was stolen.

Learning from the mistakes of the first two expeditions Hearne contrived to travel as the only European with a group of Indians led by the great chief Matonabbee. The group also included eight of Matonabbee's wives to act as beasts of burden in the sledge traces, camp servants, and cooks. This third expedition set out in December 1770, in order to reach the Coppermine River in summer, by which he could descend to the Arctic in canoes.

Matonabbee kept a fast pace, so fast they reached the great caribou traverse before provisions dwindled and in time for the spring hunt. Here all the Indian hunters of the north gathered to hunt the vast herds of caribou migrating north for summer. A store of meat was laid up for Hearne's voyage and a band of warriors joined the expedition. Matonabbee ordered the women to wait for his return in the Athabasca country to the west.

The Chipewyans were generally a mild and peaceful people, however they were in a state of conflict with the Inuit. A great number of Indians joined Hearne's party to accompany them to the Coppermine River with intent to murder Inuit, who were understood to frequent that river in considerable numbers.

On July 14, 1771, they reached the Coppermine River, a small stream flowing over a rocky bed in the "Barren Lands of the Little Sticks". A few miles down the river, just above a cataract, were the domed wigwams of an Eskimo camp. At 1am on July 17, 1771 Matonabbee and the other Indians fell upon the sleeping Eskimo in a ruthless massacre. Approximately twenty men, women and children were killed; this would be known as the Massacre at Bloody Falls.

> ...a young girl, seemingly about eighteen years of age, [was] killed so near me, that when the first spear was stuck into her side she fell down at my feet, and

> twisted round my legs, so that it was with difficulty that I could disengage myself from her dying grasps. As two Indian men pursued this unfortunate victim, I solicited very hard for her life; but the murderers made no reply till they had stuck both their spears through her body...even at this hour I cannot reflect on the transactions of that horrid day without shedding tears.

A few days later Hearne was the first European to reach the shore of the Arctic Ocean by an overland route. By tracing the Coppermine River to the Arctic Ocean he had established there was no northwest passage through the continent at lower latitudes.

This expedition also proved successful in its primary goal by discovering copper in the Coppermine River basin. However an intensive search of the area yielded only one four-pound lump of copper and commercial mining was not considered viable.

Matonabbee led Hearne back to Churchill by a wide westward circle past Bear Lake in Athabasca Country. In midwinter he became the first European to see and cross Great Slave Lake. Hearne returned to Fort Prince of Wales on 30 June 1772 having walked some 5,000 miles and explored more than 250,000 square miles.

Later Life

Hearne was sent to Saskatchewan to establish Fort Cumberland, the second inland trading post for the Hudson's Bay Company in 1774 (the first being Henley House, established in 1743, 200 km up the Albany River). Having learned to live off the land, he took minimal provisions for the eight Europeans and two Home Guard Crees who accompanied him.

After consulting some local chiefs, Hearne chose a strategic site on Pine Island Lake in the Saskatchewan River, 60 miles above Basquia. The site was linked to both the Saskatchewan River trade route and the Churchill system. He became governor of Fort Prince of Wales on 22 January 1776. On 8 August 1782 Hearne and his complement of 38 civilians were confronted by a French force under the comte de La Pérouse composed of three ships, including one of 74 guns, and 290 soldiers. As a veteran Hearne recognized hopeless odds and surrendered without a shot. Hearne and some of the other prisoners were allowed to sail back to England from Hudson Strait in a small sloop.

Hearne returned the next year but found trade had deteriorated. The Indian population had been decimated by smallpox and starvation due to the lack of normal hunting supplies of powder and shot. Matonabbee had committed suicide and the rest of Churchill's leading Indians had moved to other posts. Hearne's health began to fail and he delivered up command at Churchill on 16 August 1787 and returned to England.

In the last decade of his life he used his experiences on the barrens, on the northern coast, and in the interior to help naturalists like Thomas Pennant in their researches. His friend William Wales was a teacher at Christ's Hospital and he assisted Hearne to write *A Journey from Prince of Wales's Fort in Hudson's Bay to the Northern Ocean*. This was published in 1795, three years after Hearne's death of dropsy in November 1792 at the age of 47.

Legacy

On 1 July 1767 he chiseled his name on smooth,

glaciated stone at Sloop's Cove near Fort Prince of Wales where it remains today.

One of Wales's pupils, the poet Samuel Taylor Coleridge, made a brief notebook entry where he mentioned Hearne's book. Hearne may have been one of the inspirations for the Rime of the Ancient Mariner.

Hearne's journals and maps were proven correct by Sir John Franklin when he verified the discovery of the massacre at Bloody Falls during his own Coppermine Expedition of 1819-1822. He wrote:

Several human skulls which bore the marks of violence, and many bones were strewed about the encampment, and as the spot exactly answers the description, given by Mr. Hearne, of the place...

Hearne is mentioned by Charles Darwin in the sixth chapter of *The Origin of Species*:

In North America the black bear was seen by Hearne swimming for hours with widely open mouth, thus catching, like a whale, insects in the water.

There is a college that was built and named after him in Inuvik, Northwest Territories. A school in Toronto, Ontario was also built in his name in 1973.

23

Life and Works of Margaret Laurence

The Canadian writer Margaret Laurence (1926-1987) was the author of many novels and stories about Africa and Canada. The five Manawaka novels feature strongly etched heroines and won international acclaim.

Margaret Laurence (Jean Margaret Wemyss) was born in 1926 in Neepawa, Manitoba, Canada. Her father's family had been Scottish settlers in the district; her mother's, Irish. She was educated in Neepawa and at United College in Winnipeg, which she attended from 1944 to 1947. After graduation she worked as a reporter on the *Winnipeg Citizen,* a labor daily. In 1948 she married Jack Laurence, a civil engineering graduate from the University of Manitoba. In 1949 the Laurences went to England and in 1950 to Africa, where Jack Laurence was in charge of a dam-building project in Somaliland (now Somalia). In 1952 they moved to the Gold Coast (now Ghana), where they lived until 1957. Their daughter, Jocelyn, was born during a leave in England in 1952; their son, David, in Ghana in 1955. The Laurences returned to Vancouver, Canada, in 1957. In 1962 Margaret Laurence moved with her children to England, where she lived until moving back to Canada permanently in 1974. The

Laurences were divorced in 1969. After 1974 Margaret Laurence lived in Lakefield, Ontario, a small town near the city of Peterborough. Much of her last novel, *The Diviners,* was written at a cottage on the Otonabee River, near her home in Lakefield.

Education

In 1944, Laurence attended Winnipeg's United College (now the University of Winnipeg) on scholarship, pursuing an honours English degree. She wrote for the student newspaper and became involved with the "Old Left" socialist reform group. She graduated in 1947. Soon afterwards, she was hired as a reporter for *The Winnipeg Citizen,* where she wrote book reviews, covered labour issues, and hosted a daily radio column.

Personal life

Following her graduation from United College, she married John Fergus Laurence, an engineer. His job took them to England (1949), the then-British protectorate of British Somaliland (1950–1952), as well as the British colony of the Gold Coast (1952–1957). Laurence developed an admiration for Africa and of its various populations, which found expression in her writing.

In 1952, Laurence gave birth to daughter Jocelyn during a leave in England. Son David was born in 1955 in the Gold Coast. The family left the Gold Coast just before it gained independence as Ghana in 1957, moving to Vancouver, British Columbia, where they stayed for five years.

In 1962, she separated from her husband and moved to London, England for a year. She then moved to Elm Cottage (Penn, Buckinghamshire) where she lived for more than ten years, although she visited Canada often. Her divorce became final in 1969. That year, she became writer in residence at the University of Toronto. A few years later, she moved to Lakefield, Ontario. She also bought a cabin on the Otonabee River near Peterborough, where she wrote *The Diviners* (1974) during the summers of 1971 to 1973. Laurence served as Chancellor of Trent University in Peterborough from 1981 to 1983.

In 1986, Laurence was diagnosed with lung cancer late in the disease's development. According to the James King biography, *The Life of Margaret Laurence*, the prognosis was grave, and as the cancer had spread to other organs, there was no treatment offered beyond palliative care. Laurence decided the best course of action was to spare herself and her family further suffering. She committed suicide at her home at 8 Regent St., Lakefield, on January 5, 1987. She was buried in her hometown in the Neepawa Cemetery, Neepawa, Manitoba. Laurence's house in Neepawa has been turned into a museum. Her literary papers are housed in the Clara Thomas Archives at York University.

Literary Career

One of Canada's most esteemed and beloved authors by the end of her literary career, Laurence began writing short stories shortly after her marriage, as did her husband. Each published fiction in literary periodicals while living in Africa, but Margaret continued to write and expand her range. Her early novels were influenced by her experience as a minority in Africa. They show a strong sense of Christian symbolism and ethical concern for being a white person in a colonial state.

It was after her return to Canada that she wrote *The Stone Angel,* the book for which she is best known. Set in a fictional prairie small town, the novel is narrated retrospectively by Hagar Shipley, a ninety-four year old woman living in her eldest son's home in Vancouver. Published in 1964, the novel is of the literary form that looks at the entire life of a person, and Laurence produced a novel from a Canadian experience. After finishing school, the narrator moves from Toronto to Manitoba, and marries a rough-mannered homesteader, Bram Shipley, against the wishes of her father, who then disinherits her — disinheritance a recurring theme in much of Laurence's fiction. The couple struggles through the economic hardship and climatic challenges of Canadian frontier existence, and Hagar, unhappy in the relationship, leaves Bram, moving with her son John to Vancouver where she works as a domestic for many years, betraying her social class and upbringing. The novel is required reading in many North American school systems and colleges.

Laurence was published by Canadian publishing company McClelland and Stewart, and she became one of the key figures in the emerging Canadian literature tradition. Her published works after *The Stone Angel* express the changing role of women's lives in the 1970s. Although on the surface, her later works like the *The Diviners* depict very different roles for women than her earlier novels do, it is safe to say that Laurence throughout her career was faithfully dedicated to presenting a female perspective on contemporary life, depicting the choices — and consequences of those choices — women must make to find meaning and purpose in life.

In later life, Laurence was troubled when a fundamentalist Christian group succeeded in briefly removing *The Diviners* as course material from Lakefield High School, her local secondary school.

The Stone Angel, a feature-length film based on Laurence's novel, written and directed by Kari Skogland and starring Ellen Burstyn premiered in Fall 2007.

First Successes

Margaret Laurence started writing when she was young. Her first novel, called *Pillars of the Nation,* was written at the age of 12 for a contest sponsored by the *Manitoba Free Press.* A story about pioneer settlers of the West, its town was already called Manawaka. It won honorable mention. Throughout high school and college discerning teachers such as Mildred Musgrove and Malcolm Ross recognized in her a fiction writer's talent, but it was not until her African experiences that the talent blossomed.

Intrigued by the extensive oral literature of the Somali people, she searched out and translated examples of the folk tales, love poems, and formal, highly-developed *gabei,* gathering them together in a book called *A Tree for Poverty,* published in 1954. In Ghana she began to write the short stories later collected and published as *The Tomorrow-Tamer* (London, 1963; New York, 1964). Her first novel, *This Side Jordan* (1960), is set in Ghana, and *The Prophet's Camel Bell* (1963), published in the United States as *New Wind in a Dry Land* (1964), is a retrospective account of her experiences in Somaliland. There she came to a dawning awareness that the themes of freedom, individual dignity, and survival are universal in all literature, applicable to her own Canadian past and present as well as to the desert people of Somalia. She wrote of African people with tact and empathy, so much so that she was repeatedly praised by Chinua Achebe, the senior Nigerian novelist, for her portrayals of Africans and their dilemmas.

The Manawaka Cycle

Five works set in the Canadian prairie town of Manawaka constitute the major body of Laurence's fiction: *The Stone Angel* (1964), *A Jest of God* (1966), *The Fire-Dwellers* (1969), *A Bird in the House* (1970), and *The Diviners* (1974). In them, through the voices of five memorable women, she created a multi-faceted Canadian experience through four generations. In *The Stone Angel* Hagar Shipley tells her story of pride and pain and of learning the meaning of love just before it is too late. Rachel Cameron of *A Jest of God* is a spinster school-teacher, trapped in Manawaka by the demands of her mother and, even more, by her own fears and self-distrust. Through the crucial events of one summer she comes to a degree of self-knowledge and a limited freedom. Her sister, Stacey MacAindra of *The Fire-Dwellers,* lives in Vancouver with her husband and four children. She is battered from all sides by an urban environment that seems monstrously threatening and by the multiple demands on her as wife, mother, and friend. But Stacey is strong, a doer and an activator. In the weeks before her 40th birthday she lives through a series of shocks that brings her an increased acceptance of herself and of the irreversible process of life.

The collection of short stories *A Bird in the House* centers on the young Vanessa MacLeod, her initiation into the mysteries of love and loss, and her gradual acceptance and understanding of Grandfather Connor. As a child she feared and resented him and his tyranny; maturity brings her respect for his strengths and pity for his self-imposed isolation.

The Divinersis the story of Morag Gunn of Manawaka, a writer of novels. On one level the story unfolds the process of Morag's life from the death of her parents when she was young to the novel's present when she is 47, struggling to understand her own life and caught up in a tormenting concern for her daughter, Pique. In its deepest and broadest meaning *The Diviners* is the story of a profoundly religious pilgrimage, the affirmation of faith and the finding of grace.

The Diviners

The Diviners published by McClelland & Stewart in 1974, it was Laurence's final novel, and is considered one of the classics of Canadian literature. The novel won the Governor General's Award for English language fiction in 1974. The protagonist of the novel is Morag Gunn, a fiercely independent writer who grew up in Manawaka, Manitoba. Morag has a difficult relationship with her daughter Pique and her Métis lover Jules Tonnerre, and struggles to maintain her independence.

The Diviners was adapted for television by Anne Wheeler, with a screenplay by Linda Svendsen, and aired on CBC Television in 1993. Sonja Smits starred as Morag, and Tom Jackson starred as Jules Tonnerre.

The book has been repeatedly banned by schoolboards and high schools - usually by complaint from fundamentalist Christian groups labelling the book blasphemous and obscene. It is a regularly featured book on the Canadian Freedom to Read campaign.

Other Works and Awards

In 1968 Margaret Laurence published *Long Drums and Cannons,* a study of contemporary Nigerian novelists and playwrights, and in 1976, *Heart of a Stranger,* a collection of personal, often autobiographical essays. She also wrote four children's books: *Jason's Quest* (1970), *The Olden Days Coat* (1979), *Six Darn Cows* (1979), and *A Christmas Story* (1980). Margaret Laurence was a beloved and respected Canadian. She was awarded the Order of Canada, the Molson Prize, and honorary degrees by many universities. The Manawaka novels have been translated into many languages.

Bibliography

Adele Freedman. Review of *Visions* (E.5). *Quill & Quire* 49 (December 1983): 24.

Alan Twigg. "From Indian Legends to Feminist Mythology." *The Province* (Vancouver), 20 March 1983: Magazine, 6.

Charles Lillard. Review of *Tzuhalem's Mountain* (A.12) and *The Beauty of the Weapons* (A.14). *The Reader* (Vancouver), June 1983: 1-4.

Charles Seluzicki. Review of *Albion Broadsheets 1980-81. Fine Print* (San Francisco) 9.2 (April 1983): 51-52.

Chaviva Hosek. "Poetry in English 1950 to 1982." *The Oxford Companion to Canadian Literature,* edited by William Toye. Toronto: Oxford University Press, 1983: 667-668.

Colin Browne. "I Believe in Vengeance." *CVII* [*Contemporary Verse Two*] (Winnipeg) 5.2 (Winter 1980/81): 10-17.

Douglas Barbour. "Canadian Poetry Chronicle: vi." *Dalhousie Review* (Halifax) 58.3 (Autumn 1978): 555-578.

Gail McKay. *The Pat Lowther Poem.* Toronto: Coach House Press, 1978

Harold Town. "Critics, History and Art." *The Globe and Mail* (Toronto), 24 December 1983: Entertainment, 15. Review of *Visions* (E.5).

J.E. Simpson. Review of *Visions* (E.5). *CM* 12.5 (September 1984): 189.

Jane Munro. "Bringhurst's Range: Essential Information." *CVII* [*Contemporary Verse Two*] 5.2 (Winter 1980/81): 38-41.

Joel H. Kaplan. "Multiple Vision." *Canadian Literature* 103 (Winter 1984): 80-81.

John Biguenet. "Stones are to Silence as Darkness is to Light." *West Coast Review* (Burnaby, British Columbia) 11.2 (October 1976): 39.

Kerry Shawn Keys. "Bringhurst Aorist." *Loose Leaves Fall: Selected Poems*. Camp Hill, Pennsylvania: Pine Press, 1977: 72.

Marilyn Bowering. "Long Poems from the Little Presses." *Quill & Quire* 44.9 (July 1978): 4.

Peter Millard. Review of *Visions* (E.5). *Arts Manitoba* (Winnipeg) 4.1 (Winter 1984): 27.

Raymond J. Smith. "Poetry Chronicle." *The Ontario Review* (Windsor, Ontario) 4 (Spring/Summer 1976): 104-110. Review of several books, including *Bergschrund* (A.6).

Reginald Berry. "Natural & Unnatural." *Canadian Literature* (Vancouver) 102 (Autumn 1984): 136-138.

Robert A. Lecker. Review of *Bergschrund* (A.6). *Quill & Quire* (Toronto) 42.5 (April 1976): 46.

Robert Fulford. "By Persons Unknown." *Saturday Night* (Toronto), March 1984: 9-11.

Robin Skelton. "Poetry Selected, Collected, and Resurrected." *Quill & Quire* 49.3 (February 1983): 33.

Russell Bingham. "In-depth Look at Canadian Art." Edmonton (Alberta) *Journal*, 11 December 1983: .... Review of *Visions* (E.5).

Sam Hamill. Review of *The Beauty of the Weapons* (A.14). *Western American Literature* (Logan, Utah) 18.2 (Summer 1983): 187-189.

Sandra Djwa & Ronald B. Hatch. Review of *The Beauty of the Weapons* (A.14). *University of Toronto Quarterly* 52.4 (Summer 1983): 347-348.

Sr Anne Leonard. Review of *The Beauty of the Weapons* (A.14). *CM* (Ottawa) 11.5 (September 1983): 213.

Steven Smith. Review of *The Beauty of the Weapons* (A.14). *Books in Canada* (Toronto) 12.7 (August/September 1983): 25-27.

Susan Crean. Review of *Visions* (E.5). *Books in Canada* 13.1 (January 1984): 23-24.

W.J. Keith. Review of *The Beauty of the Weapons* (A.14). *Canadian Book Review Annual 1982*. Toronto: Simon & Pierre, 1983: 164.

Wayne Holder. Review of *The Beauty of the Weapons* (A.14). *The Vancouver Literary News* 4.83 (April 1983): 26-31.

Index